I0114627

SAIGON STORIES

iBooks
Habent Sua Fata Libelli

iBooks
Manhanset House
Shelter Island Hts., New York 11965-0342

bricktower@aol.com • www.ibooksinc.com

All rights reserved under the International and Pan-American Copyright Conventions. Printed in the United States by J. Boylston & Company, Publishers, New York. No part of this publication may be reproduced, stored in a retrieval system, or transmitted in any form or by any means, electronic, or otherwise, without the prior written permission of the copyright holder. The iBooks colophon is a trademark of J. Boylston & Company, Publishers.

Library of Congress Cataloging-in-Publication Data
De Francia, James
Saigon Stories
p. cm.

1. Biography & Autobiography—Military
2. History—Military—Vietnam War.
3. History—Asia—Southeast Asia. 4. History—Military—United States.
Nonfiction, I. Title.
ISBN: 978-1-87696-904-2, Hardcover
ISBN: 978-1-59019-010-4, Trade Paper

Copyright © 2023 by James De Francia

December 2023

SAIGON STORIES

James De Francia

Acknowledgments

The author particularly acknowledges the assistance provided by the Union League Club of New York, through its Library Committee. This was offered through the many presentations orchestrated by the Committee for authors, agents, publishers, and editors to share their experiences with Club members, who had long considered writing a book, but needed guidance on how that is accomplished. Especially noted is the assistance and encouragement of Club members Don Mazzella and Ann Marie Sabath who personally assisted this author in numerous ways!

Lastly, thanks are also noted for Vice Admiral David Robinson USN, a classmate of the author at the Naval Academy, who kindly critiqued the writing, especially for its accuracy in citing naval organizations, events, and protocols.

Dedication

This writing is dedicated to the valiant, unquestioned service of all those members of our Armed Forces who heeded their countries call, without question, in the years following these stories of Vietnam. Especially remembered among those who served are the author's Naval Academy Classmates who gave their lives in that service.

TABLE OF CONTENTS

INTRODUCTION

*H*umor, romance, and adventure do exist in the midst of any war's horror. Laughter can alleviate the sorrows of conflict, and return us to a sense of humanity.

Yet, laughter is still largely absent from our recollections of the Vietnam years.

The national memory of the Vietnam War has been very dark. This is much evidenced in films such as *Platoon, The Deer Hunter*, and *Apocalypse Now*.

By contrast, WWII produced some very light-hearted books such as *No Time for Sergeants, Catch 22*, and *Tales of the South Pacific*, the last also being a long running Broadway musical. Even the Korean conflict produced *MASH* as a laugh provoking popular TV series. All of these books and shows encompassed humor, romance, and adventure as a counter point to the sadness and tragedy brought on by those conflicts.

That, however, has not been the case with Vietnam.

There seem to be many reasons for the absence of such lighter stories associated with Vietnam. It was a socially turbulent time during which we Americans had difficulty, in our national turmoil, finding in that war anything at all that was humorous, or romantic. And though such events did occur, they have never found their way into print.

But they did happen - mostly in the period that might be thought of as "between the wars." That is, after the Vietnamese war against the French ended, and before the full-fledged Vietnamese war with the

Americans began. In that interregnum we progressively supplanted the French, following their 1954 defeat at the battle of Dien Bien Phu, (ending, after 100 years, the Vietnamese revolt against French colonial rule and instigating French departure). That departure created a progressively American quasi-colonial replacement of the prior Franco-Vietnamese cultural, political, and social environment.

The end of that French-to-American transition was the period of my own service in Saigon, and the stories that follow I have been telling friends and family for years. These are tales of a young Navy officer's early military misadventures; a young man's first real romance; clever maneuvering through the military bureaucracy; and some brash events that even caught international press attention!

As we are now commemorating the 50th year since the closure of our military engagement in Vietnam, it seemed a good time to record these tales and share them with others, as well.

My intent here is to lighten some of our memories of the Vietnam conflict. More importantly, I dedicate this writing to my Naval Academy classmates who lost their lives in dutiful service to our nation in the Vietnam years following my own experiences.

They are loved and greatly missed.

James
De Francia

CHAPTER

ONE

THE MOVIES

You never know what will happen to your
life for having gone to the movies.

And such was the first event leading to my long journey to Saigon...
...going to the movies.

It was in my last year as a midshipman at the Naval Academy. Truth be told, I was far from an ideal student. On the contrary, I broke numerous Academy rules and was considered something of a discipline problem. Indeed, I had acquired by Christmas 80% of the demerits permitted in one's last year at school. The Commandant had thus placed me in "protective custody" by restricting me to the Academy grounds for the entire second semester of my last year - January to May, 1963. The hope, and intent, was that it would limit my rule breaking opportunities.

During those five months, I was prohibited from leaving the campus or, as the Navy called it, "The Yard." When not in class, at meals, participating in a permitted athletic activity, or sleeping at night, I had to regularly report to the Battalion Office. The Commandant mandated that I show up there every two hours, reveille to lights-out taps, with the exceptions noted above.

It goes without saying that I was bored to death in what I considered to be semi-imprisonment. Sources of amusement and entertainment were scarce and I came to favor vicarious escape by watching movies within the confines of the Academy.

Luckily, a different feature film was shown weekly in a theatre hall in The Yard. Although the films were dated, they were still mostly first-tier. Having no other choice, I watched whatever was on the screen.

And so, I came to view "Saigon" a 1948 film starring Alan Ladd and Veronica Lake. I was fascinated by the women with French accents garbed in sexy dresses. When these lovely ladies weren't sipping exotic cocktails in shadowy bars, they were enticing mysterious men wearing low slung fedoras and trench coats. Everything French being romantic, and the oriental backdrop adding the exotic, the movie stayed in my mind the rest of the semester.

Following graduation from the Academy - with five allowed demerits to spare - I headed to the Navy Supply School in Athens, Georgia. There I was to learn logistics and finance during a five-month program. Completion of this curriculum would then qualify me to join the fleet as an officer in the Supply Corps.

Unfortunately, my rambunctious behavior from Academy days had not changed a bit. I was not an attentive student and still a bit of a discipline problem. My priority was to attend parties at nearby sorority and frat houses on the adjoining University of Georgia campus, and court the lovely co-eds! The result was that I soon paid the consequences for my bad study habits.

Upon completing Supply School, my colleagues and I could choose our first duty stations based on class standing. Not surprisingly, my name ranked near the bottom of the pile: 119 out of 126.

The process called for a list of open billets to be posted in early November for selection by the students, in their order of class ranking.

The Supply School staff had ingrained in us to early aspire to "independent duty." This was to serve as the sole Supply Officer on a small ship, like a destroyer. Second as an aspirational post was duty as an assistant on a larger combat vessel, such as a cruiser or an aircraft carrier. Lower on the prestige list were amphibious troop and cargo carrying ships. Lowest was shore duty.

The duty stations that ranked lowest in aspirational priority were not much sought after, as they were thought to little aide future career advancement. Such postings were considered the crumbs for those lower in Supply School class standing – like me.

But, back to the movies....I was delighted to see two available shore billets posted that early November – in Saigon! The movie seen a few months earlier came back to prominent memory. Although there was no direct U.S. military engagement in Vietnam at that time, there were limited military advisory and supply efforts supporting the South Vietnamese armed forces in the emerging conflict with the Communist North Vietnam regime.

And nothing, in the earlier part of that year, had produced much fodder for news of Vietnam in U.S. papers. At the time of Academy graduation in June, the front page of the Washington Post focused on Pope John's death, the indictment of Jimmy Hoffa for trade union fraud, and the President's calling on the top 100 business leaders in the country to address racial barriers. The New York Times echoed this coverage with the exception of a very small article on student protests in Saigon. Vietnam was not in the public forum.

As for the military, it was considered a low-profile advisory mission, with no formal "war" connotation at the time, and the two posted billets in Saigon went begging as lacking career enhancement. But I saw these billets quite differently - thanks to the movie.

Recalling the film, I envisioned Saigon to be a place of adventure, romance, and intrigue; and most certainly far more interesting than a troop ship or a supply center. The added benefit of being able to earn a campaign ribbon for serving in the Saigon billet was the clincher!

"Campaign ribbons" are awarded for service in specific theatres of military operations. There were few such locations in the comparatively peaceful post-Korea world of that day. Wintering in Antarctica was a prospect, but certainly not on my list! Vietnam, however, had a lingering designation as an operational military theatre dating from the early 1950s. Our limited assistance to the French in combating colonial (and perceived communist) insurrection had then been designated a "campaign" - and the designation remained.

While at the Academy, I had always pitied the younger officers on the staff who had no "salad dressing" on their uniforms. (The term refers to the cluster of ribbons worn on the left breast of the uniform.) Not yet in service, they had missed time in Korea, and it was since a largely peaceful world; hence no campaigns - and no ribbons. These younger officers thus lacked the splash of color which added to the glamor of the uniform. Looking good was important. Ribbons helped. Girls liked them. And Saigon offered both adventure *and* a ribbon – a "twofer."

I clearly saw the opportunity, and marked Saigon as my choice of duty station. Together with my Academy and Supply School classmate, Max, we secured the two unwanted billets in this faraway city, then of little note.

My life followed a new course – for having gone to the movies.

CHAPTER
TWO

THE JOURNEY

"It is not the destination, it is the journey."
— RALPH WALDO EMERSON

Selection of post now made, I awaited Orders as completion of Supply School neared. Duty posts were officially assigned by officers in the Bureau of Naval Personnel (BUPERS as we called it), based on the needs of the various commands but also with the expressed preferences of the candidates under consideration for new postings. These billet-controlling officers would then "detail" one to a new assignment. It was made clear that these "Detailers," as such officers were known, were to be courted. They could be persuaded and influenced, and not just deferred to as handlers, who sent us wherever they liked.

Saigon was my choice from the list of available duty assignments posted at Supply School, and the Detailer would now attend to sending my Orders.

In the month of November, however, many things changed in Saigon. These included the assassination of its President, a coup, intensified political acrimony, and much international discussion. There were growing anti-government demonstrations by both students and Buddhist monks, as well as increased terrorist attacks by North Vietnamese guerillas, and political intrigue provoked by Madam Nhu, the Dragon Lady (as she was called by the U.S. press) of the recently overthrown South Vietnamese regime. More significantly, there was also the assassination within the same month of U.S. President John Kennedy.

I soon found that all these events were about to directly impact my life. On a wintery day in early December, about to finish Supply School, I received my Orders. But rather than being sent to Saigon, they read that I would be joining an amphibious ship, an attack troop transport, in San Diego, in the role of Disbursing Officer.

Startled of course, I wondered "What happened to Saigon, and my chosen billet?" Not knowing if I should be offended or just disappointed, I quickly called the Detailer at BUPERS and asked for an explanation as to why my orders were not what I had selected from the list posted in November.

As to the reason given by the Detailer in his reply, some background......

President Kennedy had been assassinated on November 22, only days after I had made the billet selection for Saigon. The U.S. was in a leadership transition and some political turmoil. Vietnam was also in turmoil following the assassination of its President, in the course of a military coup.

Vice President Lyndon Johnson had taken office and retained the Kennedy Cabinet, yet wasted no time introducing his own policies. In the first few weeks under the new President, however, certain policies established under Kennedy were still being advanced by Robert McNamara, as Secretary of Defense, and were proceeding apace.

One such continuing policy was that the heretofore limited North/South conflict in Vietnam was seen to be winding down; or, better said, expert political and military projections showed that it would all end soon. As a consequence, the American military advisory staff was to be reduced. The two billets in Saigon were thus closed, it was explained by the Detailer.

Thus explained, orders are orders, so upon being detached from the Supply School in mid-December I headed West in my '62 white Chevy sedan to San Diego and arrived at the ship on January 13, 1964.

Upon reporting aboard I was surprised to find a letter waiting for me from Max, my Navy classmate and fellow Saigon selector. He, too, had received surprise orders at Supply School - to a repair ship in Norfolk, Virginia. We had agreed to keep in touch as we set about our Navy careers in opposite oceans. Max's letter indicated that he was still in dialog with the Detailer and would keep me posted on his success, as he was not happy with the repair ship assignment. For my part, life was also not evolving as I had expected from the movie.

I reported to my new job on the attack transport. We were making ready for a passage to the Far East, with Marines aboard. I went about learning the supply systems on the vessel, drawing cash from the local bank for use as needed in the crossing, and adapting to shipboard life. A few days later we set sail, and our first stop, after a week at sea, was in Honolulu. Visiting Hawaii was a thrill for a boy from the mountains of Colorado. Shore liberty was generously granted by the Captain and I enjoyed the many sights and venues of the city: cocktails at the Royal Hawaiian, evening luau shows with dinner, and some flirtations with young tourist girls.

After our port call, we were about to return to sea and further transit to Japan when the ship's mail arrived, the last to be expected for a few weeks. In it was another letter from Max.

He advised that he had been contacted by the Detailer and asked if he still wanted the Saigon assignment, as the post had been reactivated. The change had apparently resulted from a Washington reassessment of U.S. engagement in South Vietnam following the turmoil that emerged in the weeks following the assassination of South Vietnamese President Diem and his brother. In any event, Max advised the Detailer that he did, indeed, still want the post. He was told to stand by for new orders to Saigon, but first to attend Commissary School in New York, followed by Survival School in San Diego. The latter was a training program for jungle survival, assigned irregularly, prior to duty assignments in Vietnam.

Max knew, of course, that Saigon was also my Supply School first choice of duty station. His letter thus suggested that I again contact the Detailer, which I did immediately.

Upon calling, I was delighted to hear from the Detailer that he had been trying to contact me - unsuccessfully - but knew that I was at sea. He was planning to instead write in order to ask me the same question that had been directed to Max. "Do you still want the Saigon assignment," he asked. My response was an enthusiastic "yes!"

Saigon was back in my life. The movie revived in my memory.

As for Vietnam being in the news – it wasn't.

The January 15, 1964, front page of the NY Times headlined U.S. concerns in Panama, with riots there linked to Castro connections in Cuba; rent strikes in New York City; and a 12" snow storm the day prior. There was but one small column on Vietnam that cited the need for agricultural reform under the new military regime following the coup of the preceding November.

My current duty circumstance, however, was different than that of Max. The Detailer advised that he now needed to order another officer to fill my ship billet as Disbursing Officer. That candidate would be chosen from the next group finishing Supply School in March, 1964.

I was instructed to remain on the ship while it crossed the Pacific with the Marine battalion and I would get orders in due course to detach in the Far East and proceed to Saigon. And even better, no unpleasant Survival School!

So, I settled in for what I expected to be a leisurely sea transit to Asia as an officer in the ship's company. I would receive my Saigon orders and detach from the ship at some point in the near future.

Mindful of Ralph Waldo Emerson's advice, I decided to see what adventures might be found in the coming weeks of the journey. There were certainly a few!

As the junior Supply Officer, I was assigned to what I considered to be the easiest job on the ship: Disbursing Officer. My responsibilities centered on being the paymaster and keeper of the ship's funds. In those days, payroll was made in cash to the crew on the 15th and last day of each month. Funds were also disbursed to pay for services and supplies needed during port visits.

The ship's Supply Officer was a Lieutenant who had come up through the enlisted ranks – a "mustang" as such officers were known. The other Assistant Supply Officer, who also handled food service, was a Lieutenant, Junior Grade (a "jg"), and then me – an Ensign – serving as Disbursing Officer.

I had an experienced American Samoan 1st Class Petty Officer as my assistant. He went by "Bird," since his Samoan name was a challenge.

Before the ship left San Diego, Bird and I went to a local bank equipped with side arms and accompanied by a Marine guard. We withdrew $250,000 in cash to cover payroll and other cash needs while at sea and secured the cash in the ship's safe.

The ship soon left for points in the Western Pacific, carrying our battalion of Marines. I made my first pay day disbursements at sea on January 31st, with Bird's able eye and assistance.

I also quickly found an efficient protocol for task management. I would simply peruse my IN box each day, and put back in the OUT box anything that seemed of consequence. I then signed whatever Bird returned to my IN box. Job done! I had the utmost confidence in Bird and his judgement, but did read in more detail what he had returned. This process saved me time in not reading every detail on the first pass!

Other than pay day, I had little to do while at sea. I took advantage of the free time by getting to know a few of the crewman who collected coins. I would carefully watch as they scrutinized my ample stock of coinage for collectibles.

In order to feel more productive and look useful, I decided to approach the Captain and offer to stand deck watches, a duty otherwise relegated to line officers (as a Supply Officer, I was a staff officer). The Captain took me up on my offer after I related to him that I had scored quite well at the Academy in navigation and ship handling. I was promptly assigned as a Junior Officer of the Deck for night watches. The journey progressed.

One thing led to another. As a result of enjoying my "volunteer" job as a Junior Officer of the Deck, I decided to expand upon the experience. That included learning about amphibious assault - troop landings - which was the task of getting our Marines ashore for combat, and how that was done.

Bill, a Lieutenant in the wardroom with whom I had become friendly, managed the landing process. He instructed me that first the ship anchored off shore at the point of invasion. We would then put the landing craft that we carried into the water (the phrase "away all boats" was the order for that action). These craft, manned by a coxswain, would then circle and come along side one-by-one to receive Marines climbing down the side on cargo nets. Thus loaded, the boats would form into a line, parallel to the beach, and then turn and proceed in a "wave" to the landing site. Each wave was to be led by a Wave Commander, in a fast patrol craft of a speedboat nature with a covered cockpit, and replete with radios, whip antennas, signal flags, lights, horns, and all manner of fun stuff!

Now that sounded exciting, so I volunteered to be a Wave Commander. Given my brief experience as a Junior Officer of the Deck with favorable reviews, Bill agreed, and said that he would train me at the next landing exercise.

One week later, which was in late February, we were off the coast of Japan preparing for a landing training exercise. It was time for the fun of being a Wave Commander.

Now during the prior weeks at sea, I had been the butt of some wardroom teasing as the curious Supply Officer who actually liked night duty on the Bridge. I was also teased about being an Academy graduate, the only one among the officers aboard other than the Captain, who was assigned for "deep draft" ship experience prior to being considered for command of a carrier or cruiser. Being a Wave Commander offered an opportunity to show my friendly antagonists some military panache' as an Academy schooled warrior and seaman, my disciplinary record notwithstanding.

Anchored off the shore of Japan, preparing for landing training, I was intent on presenting myself with theatrical aplomb. First, I instructed one of the stewards serving the officers to polish my pair of combat boots to a brilliant shine. I also had my helmet polished to a silver gleam, reminiscent of General Patton in the field.

To this I added a pair of heavily starched khaki trousers, with cuffs tucked into the boots for a bloused, riding boot effect; then a smartly starched khaki shirt, and a pair of aviator sunglasses such as those favored by General MacArthur.

As though that were not enough, the finishing touch was a swagger stick, borrowed from one of the Marine officers (who still carried such accoutrement in those days) and, finally, a pipe, unlit.

We sat at anchor. The landing craft were put over the side. Marines were mustering on deck. The Wave Commander speedboats were preparing to be put into the water.

In my dramatic and hopefully impressive attire, I walked out on the deck to board my assigned speedboat and be lowered into the water. Appearing on deck, I walked smartly toward the davits where the craft awaited my boarding before being lowered, slapping my swagger stick on my thigh, pipe clenched in my teeth. I noted the astonished look of the other officers, and some very amused looks among the crewmen.

Now the speedboat itself was suspended from davits, hanging some four feet or so away from the deck edge of the ship, and was steadied with lines held by two seamen who could then pull it in to the ship's edge for stepping aboard. I strutted across the deck to so board the craft. As I approached, I noted that one of the seamen holding a line was snickering and muffling a laugh.

I turned my head abruptly, still striding to the edge, and snarled at the seaman in a deep tone saying "Snap to, there sailor...what's so funny!" Taken aback, he dropped the tethering line and snapped to attention, as did his fellow crewman.

The boat, of course, then swung away from the ships edge. I turned my head forward again, never having broken stride, and proceeded to step aboard the craft – only to find myself instead stepping into thin air and falling some 25 feet into the water!

Calls of "man overboard" rang out, a signal went to one of the other boats already in the water, which headed to pick me up. My pipe was lost, my sunglasses nearly so and askew on my head, the polished helmet floating away with the swagger stick drifting off as well.

I was hauled aboard the recovering craft in just a few minutes, wet like a puppy in a rain storm, and thoroughly diminished in stature for the duration. The Captain, of course, took me to task, but also had to restrain his amusement.

Service as a Wave Commander was no longer available. Training exercise finished, we moved on to Hong Kong for a port call, and I continued to serve as a Junior Officer of the Deck, albeit with more aggressive teasing. Five days later we anchored in Hong Kong harbor for what would be my final theatrical performance at sea.

Hong Kong was the most prized port call in the Pacific, still a British territory with a colonial government structure. English organized but Chinese priced. It offered the civilized public behavior of the British, such as waiting in line for taxis or admissions, but was otherwise more colorful in its core Hong Kong Chinese nature.

The Deck Division of the crew, responsible for the maintenance of the vessel, especially relished port calls to Hong Kong, where an entire ship would be repainted by a swarming team of young women, in exchange for being given the garbage and trash from the vessel. These famous female teams were all managed by the famed Mary Sue, a very clever Hong Kong woman. She and her female team provided nearly all visiting vessels with painting services.

And shore leave for both officers and crew was a diverse treat, with a wide ethnic array of bars, restaurants, and lovely girls.

It was to be a short port call of just five days. I enjoyed shore leave every day, and visited the British China Fleet Club, all the sites on the island, shopping, great restaurants, and lively bars.

I also had occasion to visit a Chinese family who were friends of my uncle in Denver. My uncle had met the Chinese family in Hawaii during World War II. As a lawyer, he served in the U.S. Office of Price Administration (the OPA) which monitored trade during the war. Edward Chin, my uncle's Hong Kong Chinese friend, was also stationed in Hawaii. With a British education and citizenship, his responsibilities included joint U.S.-U.K. pricing oversight. Edward's warm hospitality for lunch and tea was a delightful experience, and an educational one.

Emerson's admonition about "the journey" was offering much diversity.

On the last day of the port call, I was ashore with Bill, my Wave Commander friend. We had a very rousing night on the town. Too much alcohol, too little food.

We missed the last officer's launch back to the ship at midnight. Stranded, we found a very cheap small hotel at the waterfront; one where the surprised desk clerk asked "You want room for the WHOLE night?"

We took a room, and slept off our excess of whiskey for a few hours. Arising at 5am, we tried to figure out how we would get back to the ship which was scheduled to get underway at 8am. This proved to be a difficult task!

No launches were operating from our ship, shore leave having ended the night before, and the boats from the few other Navy vessels anchored nearby were not yet taking anyone ashore at that early hour. We quickly realized that our only choice was to hire a local small craft to ferry us out to the ship.

That proved surprisingly easy with a generous offer of U.S. dollars. We boarded a junk, one of the small native fishing and trading vessels, with an outboard engine, and headed for our anchored ship.

Transit was painfully slow, and we anxiously checked our watches every few minutes. Approaching the ship as 8am neared, we saw the side ladder gangway to a sea level platform being been taken up. How to get aboard?

We loudly hailed a crewman at the stern, who recognized us and threw over a "Jacob's ladder," a rope ladder that is hooked at the top to the ship's railing and swings free. One catches it at the bottom and climbs very cautiously, rung by rung, to the top and over the side to get on board.

Up went Bill. I waited to follow until he was aboard.

Alas, at that very moment I heard over the 1-MC (the ship's loudspeaker system) the following customary announcement: "Now all department heads make your readiness for getting underway report to the Junior Officer of the Deck on the Signal Bridge."

I then remembered that I was the assigned Junior Officer of the Deck for getting underway! Scrambling up the Jacob's ladder, I was certain that all was lost. Still in civilian clothes I saw no way for me to get to the Signal Bridge in time, even if out of uniform.

Visions of harsh consequences.

At the top of the ladder, I climbed over the rail to find waiting for me none other than the Captain. He sardonically asked, "Well, are we ready to get underway?" I replied, perhaps a little too cleverly, "I don't know sir, I just got here."

Harsh consequences followed.

Anchor aweigh, we sailed for Subic Bay, in the Philippines, a major Navy operational port in the Western Pacific. Alas, for my tardiness in Hong Kong, I was removed from further duty as a Junior Officer of the Deck and confined to my stateroom except for meals and limited time in my shipboard office. A week later we arrived at Subic. Orders for me had arrived via message with instruction to move on to Saigon, and my successor as Disbursing Officer was waiting on the pier. We went through the protocols of transferring funds and accounts, and the following morning I left the ship, met by a Navy car and driver, and headed to nearby Clark Air Force Base for transit to Saigon.

But there was to be one more adventure in the course of the journey. A classmate from the Academy was now stationed in Taipei, with his new bride, at our military mission to Taiwan. On the ride to Clark, I thought it might be fun to take a few days of vacation since my orders for reporting to Saigon were somewhat vague on timing. I decided to see what transport might be available from Clark to Taipei.

Arriving at Clark, I checked the flight board to see what was flying where, and noted that a flight was scheduled to depart for Taipei the next morning, as well as a few flights to Saigon in the afternoon.

I then proceeded to check into the Visiting Officer Quarters for the night, and found a phone from which I could call Taipei on military circuits, successfully connecting with my classmate,

I advised him that I hoped to arrive the following day and would call on arrival. He graciously said I was most welcome as a house guest, and he and his wife would check on incoming flights from Clark and pick me up, to then host me in their lovely villa in the hills outside the city. An early dinner followed in the Officer's Club at Clark, and a good night's rest.

After a light breakfast the following morning, I headed for the air transport lounge, confirmed that the flight to Taipei was still on the board for a mid-morning departure, and then approached the desk where sat a junior Air Force enlisted man handling flight processing. He asked me, simply, "Where are you going?" and I answered, simply, "Taipei."

Then came the moment of truth. He asked for my orders, which I quickly produced, and while handing them to him engaged in light, distracting conversation about the weather and on-time status of the flight. He chatted amiably, stamped the orders without so much as a glance, handed me a boarding document and wished me a pleasant trip. (This was my first experience in observing that orders were rarely read, just stamped!)

The flight left on time, with no further request for presenting orders, and I was soon at the airport in Taipei. It was then the difficulty began. The airport was a joint civilian/military complex, and all passengers needed to present their documents at Taiwanese immigration. I presented my orders.

I was startled as the immigration official said that my "papers" were not in order and I could not enter the country! The official further elaborated that since my orders were NOT to the U.S. military command in Taiwan, I was essentially a tourist and needed a visa. And while I did have a passport, I did not, of course, have a visa.

I would, he advised, be put on the next flight out. In my anxious response to this prospect, asking as to a remedy, the immigration officer suggested that I consult with the separate U.S. military transport office, also in the arrivals section of the airport, near where this encounter was taking place.

I promptly proceeded to that venue, across the lobby, and was happy to find a Navy Petty Officer manning the counter at the front of a small office. I explained my dilemma, and he asked to see my orders. Upon viewing them he quite reasonably asked: "What the hell are you doing here? You are supposed to be in Saigon."

My quick reply: "Damned if I know...the Air Force put me on this plane when I presented them with my orders at Clark." That elicited from the Petty Officer a lengthy commentary, laced with soft profanity, on the ineptitude of the Air Force.

He then advised that there was only one military flight a week to Clark, and it had just left (it was the one I come in on), and the next was 7 days hence. That, of course, suited me just fine – provided I could get into the country.

This was soon resolved with a phone call from the Petty Officer to a Chief Petty Officer at the Navy command in town. I watched the dialog which was taking place on a phone in the rear of the small office, with there being much head nodding and note scribbling. In time the Petty Officer reappeared at the counter and advised that they had found a solution. My orders would be endorsed as calling for Temporary Duty (TDY in military parlance) to the U.S. Naval Mission to Taiwan.

That would allow my entry into the country. Better still, it also allowed me to collect extra pay for the expenses associated with TDY! The Navy, I was advised, intended to relay the cost to the Air Force for their transport error, but in the meantime, I was free to enter the country and could collect the permitted TDY allowance from the local pay office at the Navy facility in the city.

And so ended this segment of the journey - with a paid vacation in Taipei. My classmate soon fixed me up with a beautiful Taiwanese by the name of Felicia Lee, and the week proved marvelous.

Emerson was right....it is not just the destination,
it is the journey.

CHAPTER
THREE

ARRIVAL

"In any performance, you first come on stage, only once."

Such was the advice of my high school theatre teacher, a Jesuit with actual experience in the profession before turning to his theological vocation. He told his budding actor students that one's first appearance should be thought out and deliberate. I considered those words as I prepared to come on stage in Saigon.

I had returned to Clark AFB from Taipei. The same Air Force enlisted clerk was at the same desk, and seemed to remember me from the week before. He remarked that I looked familiar, and again asked where I was going. "Saigon" was my reply. As in our previous encounter, he did not bother to read the orders. He simply stamped them and directed me to the flight boarding area with the needed documents.

I soon boarded an Air Force cargo flight taking a load of tires and mechanical equipment to Saigon. Seated backwards, as is the custom on military flights, I was surrounded by netting securing the cargo. I got comfortable as the plane prepared for take-off.

During the flight, I read the instructional material included with my orders. This paperwork described, for new arrivals like me, the command structure in Vietnam. It also provided general information about the city, lodging, transportation and the like. It was something of the government version of a AAA travel book.

After a brief flight, we landed at Saigon's Ton Sun Nhut Air Force Base which was located on the outskirts of the city. Exiting the plane, I made my way across the tarmac to the arrival building where I handed my orders once again to an Air Force enlisted clerk.

Orders stamped, he arranged a car and driver to take me to the Navy Headquarters. These were located in the former complex of Cie. de Fabrication du Tabac, a French tobacco company, in the 5th Arrondissement of the city. More exactly, it was designated as Headquarters, Naval Support Activity, Saigon. In military jargon it was known as HEDSUPACT.

During the car trip, I thought about the movie that had inspired me to request this Saigon billet. I had a sense of satisfaction knowing that I was finally where I wanted to be, and hoped that my experiences in this city would mirror both the adventure and romance that I had seen in the film.

The time was the Spring of 1964. It was "prewar" as Americans have come to know the period. The U.S. was yet to be filled with domestic political turmoil and social unrest. The New York Times, in April of that year, highlighted Barry Goldwater's winning the Republican Primary in Illinois; labor strife with the Sanitation Union; and the death of Rachel Carson, the author of "Silent Spring." No mention of Vietnam.

Saigon was not yet in American public focus, and was still unquestionably French in its character, with a retained essence of the colonial period.

As I was driven to the hotel, I considered the cultural atmosphere. French influence was evident in both the building architecture and the street names. There was Avenue Foch, Avenue Pasquier, Rue Croix Rouge, Rue Frere Louis and Rue Catinat. As I was soon to discover, French was the primary western language. French was the cuisine. French the beverages. French the pragmatic, yet tasteful, nature of local society.

I especially loved the wide boulevards with abundant trees. Even the narrowest streets offered shade from the tropical sun, thanks to the trees. I recognized the music of French singers Edith Piaf and Johnny Halladay coming from the sidewalk cafes, bars, and restaurants. Saigon's most popular café beverages were French-press coffee, French wine, and Pernod.

Although consumer trade, newspapers, and conversation were in French, it was with a backdrop of Asian culture and mystery. There was a colorful mix of rickshaws, hand carts and "cyclos," noisy street vendors, and lovely young women in their au dai dresses with wide straw hats. All together these added an air of Vietnamese color to a largely French city, like a perfume enhancing the scent of a flower.

The car finally arrived at the Navy headquarters, situated on Rue Hung Vuong. It was one of the comparatively few streets that lacked a French name, honoring the first Vietnamese king in about 2,800 BC. The car entered a courtyard, through an arched open gate, and drew up in front of a French styled building with high doors and tall narrow windows. As I walked in, I noticed ceiling fans, wood trimmed hallways, and office doors with brass doorknobs and glass transoms. The space itself was filled with U.S. government-issued desks and file cabinets along with other standard military stock furnishings.

A Navy Petty Officer seated at the entry desk greeted me politely, standing, as I was an officer. I handed him my orders, and he dutifully stamped them. Then he prepared a packet of still more detailed local information, while asking about my journey. When he handed me the packet, he advised that I read it carefully so that I would understand the nuances and relationships of the city and the military facilities.

Since we were in a city and not on a military base, it called for different protocols for access, security and the like. The Petty Officer explained that I would be assigned temporary lodging until permanent housing was available.

I then asked if Max had yet reported for duty. My assumption was that he had likely arrived two or three weeks earlier based on our prior correspondence. After checking a few rosters, the Petty Officer informed me that Max had indeed arrived, and had just moved to his assigned permanent quarters.

The Petty Officer then provided me with a "chit" that I was to present to the local hotel as payment for what would be my temporary housing. He also informed me that my permanent quarters would be available in about two weeks.

The car provided by the Air Force had left, so the Petty Officer called for a Navy car, and the driver took me to the hotel. It was The Majestic, located on the Saigon River water front at the foot of Rue Catinat, in the 1st Arrondissement. An older, very elegant property of distinct French Riviera style, built in 1925 by a wealthy Chinese. It still retained a unique character, and was also used by Air France for its flight crews. I especially liked that aspect, seeing that these crews included lovely female French flight attendants.

Things were beginning even better than I had hoped!

As I was checking into the hotel, I realized that I had no local currency, just U.S. money. I asked the desk clerk if he could exchange some dollars. He seemed surprised at the request, but exchanged some $20 bills for Vietnamese piasters at the published official rate. Then he discreetly suggested that for future currency exchanges, I should visit the Indian booksellers next door. I quickly grasped the meaning and left him a generous tip before going to my room.

The hotel room was quite large with a comfortable sitting area, small desk, and private bath. The decor was French period furniture, with heavy drapes framing the tall windows, wall paper marked with a small fleur de lis, and framed photos of French country scenes. If I didn't know better, I would have thought that I was in Paris!

Given the comfort and ambiance of both room and hotel, I was pleased that this would be my new home for at least a fortnight. Unpacked and settled in, I left my room to take a walk around the neighborhood. Before leaving the hotel, I stopped by the front desk to quietly ask the clerk if there was a special procedure I should follow for exchanging my U.S. currency at the Indian booksellers.

The desk clerk softly explained the process. After walking into the shop, I was to browse the book selections. I was also to be aware of anyone who might be in the shop looking around or showing suspicious behavior.

When I felt comfortable that no one was watching, I was to pick up a book, any book. Then I was to cautiously slip the U.S. dollars that I wanted to exchange among the pages and take the book to the Indian clerk at the counter.

The hotel desk clerk emphasized that I was to simply hand the book with the dollars in it to the Indian, without saying a word. In turn, the Indian would discretely remove the dollars from the book and replace them with piasters at the much higher rate of about four times the official exchange. And the bonus would be that I would get to keep the book!

I was told that the Indian clerk would give me the book in a paper wrapping thanking me for the "purchase." Then off I should go!

The hotel clerk had also advised me to wait to open the wrapping and remove the piasters until I was several blocks from the shop, or better still, in another venue, such as a café.

As instructed, I followed the process and found myself generously funded with local currency. Quick math said that I could obviously benefit with this exchange on a regular basis such that my monthly Ensign's pay would be increased four-fold for local use. Together with the inexpensive cost of living in Saigon, this promised to allow me to live very comfortably.

Life in the city was off to a good start!

During my neighborhood walk, I discovered a movie theater, sidewalk cafés, bars, and restaurants. I also stumbled upon shops offering clothing, jewelry, shoes, watches, tobacco products, newspapers, and, of course, books.

Now with an understanding of my surroundings, I returned to the hotel and enjoyed a quiet dinner followed by an after-dinner drink with three lovely Air France flight attendants.

Before going to sleep that night, I decided that my goal for the following day was to find Max.

I had made my stage debut, and life in Saigon,
soon to be worthy of the theatre, had begun.

CHAPTER

FOUR

QUARTERS

"Where to bed has become, for me, to be in a place of luxury."

— NAPOLEON

Lving in the Hotel Majestic was both luxurious and quite comfortable. Breakfast was served daily in my room, consisting of coffee, fresh juice, chocolate eclairs, and fruit. Daily maid and laundry service were provided. I especially enjoyed my evening meals in the dining room at what quickly became a regular table. And with all those Air France flight attendants, I would have been happy for this to remain my permanent quarters!

As for news about Vietnam on the home front, there was none. An April edition of the New York Times had one brief column, at the bottom of the front page, concerning Saigon. It reported on the integration of the Military Advisory Group into the overall Military Assistance Command. This was said to be in the interest of administrative efficiency, with the 16,000 service members then stationed there being increased "slightly" to no more than 17,000. Notably, however, the 14 General officers then posted in Saigon were being reduced to 12. Vietnam was not a topic of great interest in the U.S. press.

In any event, in about 2 weeks I expected to be assigned a room in The Rex. This was a hotel requisitioned by the military to house officers unaccompanied by wives and family. The officers so assigned were of junior and middle grade rank, from all the services. The more senior officers, with families, were allotted private homes elsewhere in the city. Among those were the above noted dozen General officers. The most senior was an Army officer, General Harkins (soon to be succeeded by General Westmoreland), and a number of others: 6 Brigadier Generals, 4 Major Generals, and 1 Lieutenant General. The joke among the troops was that in having 12 Generals, only two more were needed to put a squad (14 soldiers) in the field!

For its part, the Navy had no Flag officer present (i.e. an Admiral) and the senior Navy officer was a Captain, who was in command of the Naval Support Activity, the unit to which both Max and I were assigned.

HEDSUPACT, as it was known, managed and maintained all the physical and support facilities in the city for all the services. That included housing, offices, storage warehouses, the motor pool and a fuel depot. In addition, the Navy managed the Commissary and the Exchange, the Officer's Clubs, and the port facilities for receipt of military cargo intended either for our own advisory forces or, mostly, for the South Vietnamese Army. In the local vernacular, it was said that while the Army ran the country, the Navy ran the city...and the Air Force got to run Ton Sun Nhut air base!

With the Generals housed very comfortably in large homes previously used by the French governing class, and the next-senior-grade officers in smaller but no less comfortable houses, the remaining officers were barracked in requisitioned hotels, such as The Rex.

First built in 1927 as the Banier Auto Hall for showing and selling Citroen cars, The Rex had been rebuilt in 1959 by a Vietnamese family. It was now a 100-room hotel over the former auto hall, which hall now housed three cinemas, a dance hall and a café. Perhaps signaling the future, the first guests, in late 1961 as renovation was finishing, were 400 American soldiers billeted for a week or two while awaiting their tent camps to be established at the airbase. They had a BBQ Thanksgiving dinner on the roof terrace, which in time would become an officer's club.

Shortly after his arrival, Max had been assigned a room there, and I was presumed to soon follow. It would be a sad day having to bid adieu to the luxury of The Majestic! As you might expect, after four years of student quarters at the Academy, followed by similar "student" accommodations at the Supply School, I was sorely disappointed with, yet again, dormitory-like living conditions as permanent quarters.

But the disappointment was about to be corrected as Max had already been in search of better living arrangements. Having arrived nearly 3 weeks ahead of me, and of similar sentiment, he had gone quickly in pursuit of a more genial place in which to bed. Thanks to these early efforts, and good fortune, we had found a house to rent within days of my arrival.

A lovely lady was involved.

While Max was lodged at The Majestic, before my arrival, he had daily frequented one of the café's on Rue Catinat. There he had met Jacqueline Zephir, a lovely woman of Indian, Chinese, and Nepalese heritage. She had just turned 30 in age, and was exotically attractive. French was her language of choice. Max, as fortune would have it, had studied French at the Academy and was quite proficient, and he courted Jacqueline gently in the ensuing days.

He learned that she was recently divorced from an executive at the Hong Kong & Shanghai Bank, had no children, and lived in an apartment in the city. For her part, I speculated, Jaqueline was a bit lonely following her divorce, was aware of the emerging social changes given the French departure, and hence found Max an attractive young American to help ease her transition.

A few days before I had arrived, Max was at dinner with Jacqueline one evening. When she asked where he was living, he replied that "for now" he was lodged at the Rex. She asked, in French, why he used the word "maintenant" ("now"), and on that choice of a word things quickly changed. Max answered that he had used "maintenant" because he was looking for a place to rent, together with me, his friend and classmate, soon to join him.

Jacqueline offered that her aunt owned a very comfortable small house in Cholon, the dominantly Chinese sector of the city in the 4ᵗʰ Arrondissement. (Saigon, like all French cities, was divided into several Arrondissements for governance purposes, and that structure continued even after the end of formal French rule.) The house, she was advised, was available for rent, and at a very good price.

Just a few days following my arrival, Max and I accompanied Jacqueline to see it.

The neighborhood was very dense with buildings of various shapes and sizes situated cheek-by-jowl. This was common in most middle-class areas of the city. But the area was clean, well-lit at night, and surprisingly quiet. It appeared safe, and Jacqueline assured that this was the case. The neighbors were mostly Chinese, interspersed with a few Vietnamese families. Max and I, the sole Westerners in the area, became immediate objects of attention.

The house was charming. It was situated at a corner intersection of two very short streets, just off the Boulevard des Marins. The neighborhood was bounded by this Boulevard on the north and by the Arroyo Chinois about three blocks to the south, a narrow water passage adjacent to the shipping canal.

Designed in a Mediterranean style, it had a light stucco exterior, large windows, tile floors and a tasteful entry at the corner of the building in the angled, cut-corner style so common in Paris. This corner entry opened into a small foyer, with a marble floor and marble staircase to the upper levels. The foyer, in turn, opened to a combined living and dining room to the left. Directly ahead was the kitchen, and a small coat closet was under the stairway.

There were two bedrooms on the second floor. One was to the left of the stair landing, larger than the other, which was to the right. The smaller one, however, benefited from a balcony (over the main entry) with warm natural light through the balcony's French doors. At the end of the short hallway was a bath and toilet, generous in size but with only cold running water, a small tub, and no shower. The kitchen was ample and well equipped with a stove, oven and sinks, as well as a good-sized refrigerator and lots of shelving. Off the kitchen were two very small servant's rooms and a tiny toilet and bath.

The third floor was actually a roof garden. One entered through a door as the stairway ended. There was no landing. We were told that the roof was really never used, and it was closed securely with a metal accordion door on the inside, and a conventional wooden door on the outside, both locked.

The rent, when allowing for the Indian bookseller's exchange rate, was a bargain.

We took it!

Our next task was to furnish the place, and for Max to quietly exit The Rex, while I concluded my short stay at The Majestic. The furnishing part proved rather simple, considering our now assigned official duties at HEDSUPACT.

Oh, and there was one small detail, but of little concern......the house was haunted!

We had found a place of at least modest luxury in which to bed.

CHAPTER
FIVE

DUTIES

"The creative exercise of duty can bring unexpected rewards."
— WITHERSPOON

*H*aving secured lodging, the next order of business was to focus on our specific duty assignments. Those assignments, it turned out, were actually several duties. In military parlance, one had a primary assignment and then "collateral" duties, which equated to additional jobs.

My primary assignment was to serve as the Supply Officer to a Detachment of Navy SeaBees, an element of a Naval Construction Battalion (hence "C" "B" and thus "SeaBees") of the Navy Civil Engineering Corps. The Detachment's mission was to maintain and operate the local buildings occupied by the U.S. military in the city, including the residential properties, as well as to provide other facility support services. These other services included the motor pool and its many vehicles, including sedans, pickup trucks, large cargo trucks, and some buses. The pool also included heavy fork lifts and earth moving equipment. And there was a fuel depot in the mix, as well, located on the outskirts of the city. Also included were generators and shipping containers, "Conexes" as they were commonly known.

My responsibilities were to assist in managing all these assets and services, with focus on cost allocation, funding, budget control, inventory, and supplies. Also included was oversight of the extensive stock of household furnishings and equipment for the quarters occupied by the senior officers and their families, as well as equipment and furnishings for the several military offices.

In addition, I was to serve as the Stevedoring Officer, which entailed overseeing the contract for the labor that off-loaded ships delivering cargo for military use. The cargo was primarily destined for the South Vietnamese Army, but also included some material for the U.S. Advisory Mission.

Max, for his part, was assigned as the Assistant Commissary and Exchange Officer. His responsibilities included oversight of acquisition and distribution of food, liquor, and all manner of consumer products, very few of which were readily available from local sources.

It was quickly apparent that our respective duty posts offered considerable opportunity to cultivate influence and privilege well beyond what might be expected by two very junior officers; in fact, the most junior officers in the entire command. There was clearly benefit to be derived from an ability to provide select services and do favors. And that, in turn, immediately suggested an ability to improve our own living conditions. Between the two of us, we had access to, and a considerable control over, nearly all the military facilities and services available in the city!

One equally beneficial collateral duty, assigned to each of us, was that of being a Sector Warden for a designated section of the city. A Warden's duty was to manage evacuation in the event of crisis. Our assigned sectors were those where the Generals and their families were housed. This assignment required a personal monthly visit to each family (i.e. the wives) of these General officers, and a briefing on the protocols of what to do if an evacuation were ordered. The intent was that these procedures remain in the forefront of each family members daily affairs.

As a consequence of these regular visits, Max and I soon became friends with the wives of all the Generals. I would call on Mrs. Harkin, and later Mrs. Westmoreland, who would invite me to join her for coffee during each visit. Max received similar hospitality when calling on other General's wives. And while no evacuation was ever ordered, these personal acquaintances proved quite helpful in the success of another event of considerable consequence some months later.

One particular benefit of our official duties, however, was immediately to be realized. Our quarters were now to be the rented house in Cholon, and it needed furniture and other essentials to make it habitable. How convenient that my duties now included the inventory control and distribution of such items!

The day after Max and I rented the house, I surveyed the Navy's residential inventory with a 2nd Class Petty Officer, who managed the warehouse in question. We picked all the needed furnishings including beds, chairs, tables, lamps, rugs, armoires, linens, table ware, cooking ware, glasses, a candelabra, and flatware - effectively everything one needed to completely furnish and equip a modest sized house. The Petty Officer asked for what residence these were intended, and I simply replied "a new one." He prepared the inventory and requisition, I advised the address, and signed it. It was simply designated on the form as "Navy officer housing."

The following morning the complete selection was loaded onto a Navy flatbed trailer truck, which departed the warehouse with the Petty Officer following in a pickup with six coolies. I led in my own car, with my driver. We all arrived at our new house in Cholon, where I directed the unloading of all the items.

While supervising the delivery, the Petty Officer asked who would be living there. I told him that Max and I were the residents. He was clearly surprised, but made no comment. I winked and said if he ever encountered any problem or question he need only refer it to me, as he was absolved of any direct responsibility. I also assured him there would not be any problem, as it was all properly accounted for with the signed inventory.

Nothing more was ever said as the Petty Officer and I continued to work together taking care of the Generals, or rather their wives, in the coming months. There was always a request from one or another of these wives for a new this-or-that, and I was sure to always quickly accommodate such requests.

As one might suspect, given my motor pool duties, I had also undertaken to assign myself a car and driver. My justification was that I was overseeing things in diverse locations. There was stevedoring in the port, household goods and Conexes in the warehouse yards, visits to the General's quarters for evacuation briefings, as well as visits to the fuel depot just outside the city, and matters of a miscellaneous nature in varied locations. There was no objection when I nonchalantly brought up the subject to my immediate superior, a Lieutenant, who implicitly agreed without discussion. I then just signed all the needed paperwork myself.

The Vietnamese driver I chose was Loi, who had briefly picked me up from The Rex each morning. He was very amiable and while weak with English, very capable in French. He now called for me at our house in Cholon, either in a sedan or a pickup truck, depending on our planned activity for the day.

I also arranged for Max to have similar transportation privileges. My justification for him was that besides needing to visit families as a Sector Warden, he made frequent visits to the port on matters related to incoming Exchange and Commissary shipments. He also had to regularly visit a cold storage unit at a remote leased facility.

Of course, we each had assigned office spaces. Mine was of moderate size, in a small light-industrial compound of prior French use. It housed offices for several SeaBee officers and sailors. It was also the storage venue for a variety of equipment, and the motor pool parts inventory shop.

Max was situated in the Commissary/Exchange complex in a comfortable office.

My assistant, Ricky, was an Army Quartermaster Specialist 4. He handled all the paperwork, of which there was much. We did a lot of inter-service support, which involved some complex accounting. The Army did it one way, the Air Force another, and then there was the Navy way. Ricky was a bright young man, just 20 years old. He aspired to be an officer and had applied for both West Point and Army ROTC appointments. In both cases he was to receive glowing recommendations from me.

After a week of settling into our new house in Cholon, I encountered my first challenge in my new post. A SeaBee Chief Petty Officer approached me with a dilemma. Our commanding officer, "Captain K" as he was known, had directed the SeaBees to dig a large decorative fish pond in the garden to the rear of his rented French house, to include underwater colored lights. They were also to install Tivoli lights on poles throughout the garden, as well as some colored flood lights in key corners. All this, of course, was to enhance the entertainment use of the ample and lovely garden for cocktail parties and outdoor dinners. Captain K was a bachelor in his mid- 40s. Dashing and charming, and as the senior naval officer, quite involved in the social circuit of Saigon. He also had an eye for the ladies, and he entertained often.

The Chief was perplexed as how to account for this significant improvement to the leased French house. He shared that concern with the Captain, who simply told him to resolve the matter and get on with the work. None of the standard job accounts seemed to apply, and the Chief was certainly not prepared to tell Captain K that it could not be done.

The Chief's stress and discomfort were quite apparent. I told him to leave it to me to find a solution. Meanwhile, he should proceed to make the preparations for starting the work while I sorted out the job accounting. The next morning, I called on him in his office in the SeaBee compound with the needed job cost instructions. The work was to be charged as "security lighting and a protective moat." To this day that work order is probably still working its way through the Defense Department accounting systems, searching for a home!

In the event, I became good friends with the Chief, who shared with Captain K that I had cleverly addressed the funding particulars (without elaboration) and I thus also became a favorite of the Captain. He called me to his office and expressed his delight at my prompt research and decision making with regard to the cost accounting, and asked where I was billeted. That gave me the opportunity to secure at least implied permission for the lodging which Max and I had just secured. I explained our recent house rental and move from the Rex. He nodded without comment, and a slight smile, and soon included both me and Max as guests at some of his social gatherings.

As the result of creatively addressing the lighting and fish pond request, we came to enjoy privileged access to our commanding officer, and a unique living arrangement.

Life in Saigon continued to improve with the creative
exercise of duty.

CHAPTER
SIX
SHOPPING

"To visit stores and buy merchandise...." — WEBSTER

Shopping was certainly an odd military assignment. But it was an assignment nonetheless and so carried out with diligence.

Just a couple of weeks after my first duty performance in finding the accounting solution for Captain K's fish pond and outdoor lighting, another creative assignment arose. This actually resulted from Max seeking a short leave for a visit to Bangkok. We were both intent on seeing as much of Southeast Asia as we were able in what was an expected one-year duty posting. Things were quiet and in good order with the Commissary and Exchange operations, so Max thought it an opportune time for a short break to visit Thailand. I did not plan to accompany him, as I had slightly less time on station and seeking a leave, however short, seemed impolitic.

Max filed the request and was then called by a Lieutenant, Beau by name, who served as Aide to Captain K. Beau, in his soft Southern drawl, asked Max if he was the officer who was quartered with me, the new Ensign that had addressed Capitan K's fish pond and lighting dilemma. Max answered that he was, indeed, my housemate.

Beau then suggested that both Max and I could visit Bangkok, and not on leave but under orders and with TDY pay to cover our expenses. Not surprisingly, Max found that to be a remarkable turn of events. Beau said that he would also accompany us and that the "mission" was to secure some new household furnishings and art work for Captain K's new quarters (the site of the fish pond and lighting). Captain K, it seemed, found the products from Thailand to be of higher quality and better taste and finish than those available from current Navy stock or local sources. Beau added that there would likely be some special requests from the Generals' wives, as well. And he concluded by advising Max that it was expected that I knew how to handle the various charges and accounting.

Max called my office with this surprising news, and shortly thereafter Beau also called, affirming the assignment. The trip was set for a few days hence, via Navy plane which would drop us off and then return six days later to pick us up.

Orders were cut, and Max and Beau set about making the hotel and transportation arrangements. I was charged with attending to the purchasing details for the assignment.

My first stop was a visit with Captain K to get a better understanding of what he wanted for his house. Along with a SeaBee Petty Officer, I visited his quarters and did a walk-through. There was need for some art work to cover a number of wall spaces, some smaller corner tables, a few lamps, a rug or two to soften the tile floors, and a few curtain fixtures for the large parlor, as well as for the dining room.

Beau had also produced a list of some items desired by a few of the Generals' wives, and these were much the same. An art piece or two for foyers, silk lamp shades, larger framed pictures for dining rooms, and some smaller rugs. (Capitan K, prudent as always, felt that adding the General's needs to his own was in good form.)

My next chore was how to implement the purchase. Some quick research found suitable accounts for the housing inventory, with the assistance of my 2ⁿᵈ Class Petty Officer friend. But that left the question of how to make these purchases in Thailand when we were at a Vietnam military post? Consultation with Beau resulted in my learning that the Air Force was the dominant U.S. presence in Bangkok, with an air command based there at the Don Muang Royal Thai Air Base in Bangkok. As it happened, there was an Air Force Major in Saigon for whom I recently had done a favor related to a ground transport matter. I promptly called upon him for some guidance. From the Major, and his Air Force supply sergeant, I learned that the process was actually somewhat simple. I just needed to take a Navy Purchase Order issued in Saigon to the Air Force Purchasing Office at the air base in Bangkok. That office would then issue purchasing orders so as to acquire the needed items and pay for them locally, charging them against the Navy purchase order.

The next item of business was to then secure the Navy Purchase Order. It was for an amount beyond my own level of authority, being for an estimated $10,000. As a consequence, I requested it of the senior Navy Supply Officer, a Commander, and advised him of the purpose. He was hesitant. I said that he could certainly call Captain K directly, if he chose, or else I could have the Captain's aide, Beau, confirm the planned program.

He chose the latter, prudently.

Beau then called, and assured the Commander that this was all at the direction of the Captain, and added that it also addressed some General's needs. Not surprisingly, the Commander saw to it that the Purchase Order was forthcoming. Meanwhile, both Max and I visited with the General's wives in question to better grasp what they felt was needed for their quarters.

All now in place, Max, Beau, and I left on a Navy C-47 a few days later and soon landed in Bangkok at the Royal Thai Air Base. Through my Air Force Major connection in Saigon, I had arranged for an Air Force car for the duration of the trip, and it took us to the Mandarin

Oriental hotel. This grand property, since its opening in 1876, was THE place to stay in the city. As we were now traveling on paid orders, we had chosen to splurge, and the hotel's quality service staff proved quite helpful to our mission.

After checking and settling in, we promptly returned to the Air Force Purchasing Office on the base. This unit had been previously alerted by message from Beau. The Navy Purchase Order was intentionally vague, and it simply stated that it was for certain "habitability" items not available in Saigon. With the Air Force officer on duty, we mutually concluded that the easiest way to address this process was to take a cash draw, then return with receipts and evidence of the goods to close the draw account. And we also agreed that draws in smaller amounts each day was the most prudent. We would call each morning for a draw and settle all the draws in full at the end of the trip.

Now organized and funded, we set about enjoying the city and attending to our shopping. The concierge at the hotel recommended a delightful young woman from a Thai architecture firm to assist us. We met her for dinner that evening and set up a schedule for the next few days. We would draw funds early each day, shop in the morning, then stop for lunch, while the morning's purchases would be placed in secure storage at the hotel. The afternoon would then be spent sightseeing, followed by dinner. On the last day of the trip we would arrange for Air Force vehicles to take us and the goods first to the Purchasing Office to settle accounts, and then to the base line for the flight back on the Navy C-47.

The assignment progressed as ordered, albeit with the local Air Force staff most curious at this Navy officer team charged with shopping! We settled accounts the last morning (with a few dollars left to spare), headed for the Navy plane with a small truck following full of the goods, and had a smooth flight back. With guidance from the young architect, and our own considered taste, we had made what turned out to be excellent choices in the goods. Captain K, and more importantly the Generals' wives, were all quite pleased with the quality and character of the desired items. These were all dutifully entered into the inventory of household goods, of course.

Max and I then enjoyed still further enhanced reputation as being the "go to" officers in the command, for requests of whatever nature.

Shopping, while an unusual military assignment, seemed career enhancing.

CHAPTER
SEVEN
SETTLING IN

"A dinner lubricates business." — Baron Stowell

Well, there we were, Max and I. We had been only a few weeks in Saigon and were already settled in a beautifully furnished, charming house. Adding to our comfort, we each had assigned cars and drivers. And we also had a French speaking household staff of two: sisters Thi Hai and Thi Ba.

The servants had been secured for us by Jacqueline, shortly after moving into the house. Their Vietnamese names were not quite clear. Thi was a female term applied as a middle name, and Hai and Ba were numbers: two and three. It seemed that these names referred to the order of female family siblings; that is, daughter number two and daughter number three. They saw no need to tell us their surnames. As Max and I understood it, the full name might have flowed as Leu Thi Ba, meaning the third daughter in the Leu family. As the surname was seemingly not important to them, they just became Thi Hai and Thi Ba to us.

Since both young women were fluent in French, it became the household language. They also brought their small dog named Gitan ("Gypsy"), which added to our domestic ambiance. Thi Ba was the cook, and very skilled at preparing French cuisine. Thi Hai handled the other domestic chores of cleaning, laundry, and general housekeeping. Thi Ba shopped daily for fresh food to prepare our dinner each evening as well as what was needed for our breakfast the following morning. Max and I both lunched at the Officer's Club or at restaurants near our offices.

Our respective drivers picked us up each morning. After arriving at our offices, we devoted our time to the various duties with which we were charged. I would frequently visit the port. Max, for his part, would address the seemingly endless special requests for Commissary and Exchange items: this Commander wanted a certain scotch; that Colonel wanted particular cigars; this Major wanted a particular ice cream; that Lieutenant wanted particular socks; and so it went.....the Generals' wives also kept us busy with requests for furnishings as well as for certain food items, wines, and liquors.

Now and then we would receive the odd special request. One, that I recall, was from a Lieutenant Commander who was an avid ham radio operator. His complaint was that he could not get good signals on his set on the third floor of The Rex. To improve his ham radio reception, I arranged for electricians from the SeaBee unit to install a wire from his window to an antenna installed on the roof; charged to "command communications."

Creative accounting. Problem solved. Friend made for future needs of a favor.

Another particular special request was from Captain K. He wanted white wall tires on his sedan. And he also wanted white cotton seat covers, and a red spot light and a low range siren to speed things up in traffic. Charged to "transportation security enhancements."

Meanwhile, on the social front, I was admitted to the Cercle Sportif, which was the local French country club, albeit lacking golf. The focus instead was on tennis, squash, croquet, swimming, lawn bowling, bridge, fine dining and a very well stocked bar. Unfortunately, there were almost no young French girls in my age group, which minimized romantic pursuits. What was enhanced, however, were my French language skills.

I did meet a lovely young British woman at the Cercle. She was, at 26, a bit older than me, and was serving with the UN Technical Assistance Bureau. She was the niece of Lord Soames, the last British Governor of Rhodesia, and had the exotic name of Sabine. After taking her to dinner a few times, I learned that she was being aggressively courted by the moderately older (in his 30s) cultural attache' in our Embassy, so I dropped the pursuit - likely before being dropped, as she was cultured and educated well above my social station! But it was a courtship learning experience nonetheless, and she was quite beautiful and charming.

Meanwhile, Max had settled into a "relationship" with Jacqueline. Oftentimes she invited friends to join us for dinner with the hope that I might connect with one of these ladies in due course. Max and I also began regular entertaining. Hosting dinner parties became a weekly event. We would extend invitations to officers whom we liked, as well as to members of the American Embassy staff and from UN agencies then still in the city. Thanks to Thi Ba's marvelous culinary skills our guests always looked forward to attending.

To our surprise, our reputations grew in the expanded international community of Saigon. The conversations during our dinners were always lively. Topics ranged from local ex-patriot affairs, to speculation on the course of Vietnamese tensions between North and South, to books and films, and to the evolving turbulence of life in Saigon amid increasingly frequent coups d'etate by Vietnamese generals. Our reputations as hosts became better known following each dinner party.

One such dinner party, however, did take an odd twist. We had invited a newly arrived Navy Lieutenant to join us for a dinner. We met him over cocktails at the Officer's Club. He seemed personable and had just taken up some administrative post in the Navy headquarters. Having been assigned to The Rex, as were nearly all officers without families, he was surprised that Max and I lived not at The Rex, but in a house in the city.

Shortly after our meeting, he approached Captain K to ask if he might also secure such lodging.

Captain K succinctly told him "No."

Asking why, Captain K replied: "Because I said so."

The Lieutenant than asked how it was that Max and I were allowed to live in private quarters.

Captain K replied: "Because I said so."

The conversation apparently then ended.

We met the Lieutenant again not long after this exchange, and he queried us further about our unique living arrangements. We refrained from elaborating as to how our housing situation had come about and instead issued an invitation to a forthcoming dinner party. This, we thought, might ease his obvious irritation. That, however, proved a miscalculation! We were soon to learn the depth of the Lieutenant's displeasure at being restricted to The Rex while two much junior officers, namely Max and me, enjoyed separate city quarters.

Following what seemed a pleasant dinner party at our house, this Lieutenant went the next day directly to the warehouse which handled the government furniture. It was still managed by the 2nd Class Petty Officer who I had befriended early on. Apparently while dining at our house, the Lieutenant took note of our furnishings, which were clearly of the style used to outfit the homes of the senior officers. He sought to confirm with the Petty Officer that ours were, in fact, government furnishings. Well, they were of course, as the Petty Officer so confirmed.

The Lieutenant, apparently in a pique of envy, then ordered the Petty Officer to immediately pick up all the furnishings at our house (an official requisition in the file notwithstanding) and return them to the warehouse post haste, insisting that our abode was not government quarters. The Petty Officer dutifully acknowledged that he would do so.

I learned all this when the Petty Officer walked into my office to inform me of the order and his need to obviously obey it. I quickly advised him that he should, of course, obey the order. But, I asked, wasn't the order explicitly "to remove the present furnishings"? He confirmed that it was.

Fine, I added, "...then have the truck also deliver new furnishings from the stock that just arrived a few days ago." As per both orders, then, the existing furnishings were to be removed and concurrently replaced with new ones. "When finished," I directed the Petty Officer, "simply confirm to the Lieutenant that you have carried out his order."

The Petty Officer was understandably nervous about this sequence of action. I convinced him that he was obeying a later order from me, while also conforming to the prior explicit order of the Lieutenant. I also reminded him that the original requisition remained on the record, so he had nothing to fear. More importantly, I assured him that the Lieutenant would never again darken our doorstep, nor would Max and I ever otherwise engage him socially, so that in time all would be forgotten.

The following day we had a house full of fresh furnishings with the old ones carted away. Nothing more ever came of the affair, as the Lieutenant was soon moved up-country to a different post. Max and I, though, became more prudent in our future invitations.

And we were also becoming more aware of the spirit haunting the house, which was starting to become an irritation.

Shortly after this affair, we had another interesting event that followed from the dinner party. In this case it involved a Mr. Xu, a Chinese friend of Jacqueline, who had joined us.

Dinner, it seems, had lubricated a business prospect.

————◆•◆•——————

CHAPTER
EIGHT
FAVORS

Favor: "To oblige, aid or facilitate." —WEBSTER

A few days following our dinner, Mr. Xu asked to meet me and Max for coffee. He suggested that we might be able to assist him with a personal matter. Given his charm at our dinner party, and Jacqueline's assurance that he was an honest and generous man, we decided there was no harm in hearing what he had to say.

We joined him at a small café near the waterfront in the late afternoon. After making small talk about our party and guests, he got to the point as to why he wanted to meet.

"As you may know, I am Hong Kong Chinese, and am in Saigon temporarily to pursue business prospects," he said. "While I am here, I would like to have a few 'personal effects' brought into the country from Hong Kong. I am suspicious, however, of the Vietnamese customs agents," he continued, "and fear they will either tax or delay entry of these personal effects," he said, adding, "You may or may not know that the Chinese and Vietnamese have a long history of antipathy."

"I wanted to meet with you," he continued, "to avoid that circumstance. My request is to ask if I might have them shipped directly to one of you." And then he added "I would be most grateful and assure you that I will 'return the favor.'"

Max and I looked at each other, almost reading each other's minds. Apparently, our reputation preceded us with regard to "arranging things." It also appeared that Mr. Xu was well aware that I served as Stevedoring Officer in the port. "My items," he had said, "will be arriving by ship."

Max spoke up and asked "Why by ship, Mr. Xu, if this will be just a single small shipment of 'personal effects'?" Mr Xu went on to explain, "I have a good friend in the French shipping company of the vessel in question. He offered to do me a favor with free transport. It will be just one medium sized crate."

Max and I excused ourselves from the table briefly to discuss the matter further. We came to the decision that since Mr. Xu was a friend of Jacqueline, and that his shipment would just contain "personal effects," we would agree to accommodate his request. We had also both clearly heard that he would "return the favor," albeit uncertain what that might entail, a favor owed is a favor of value!

Max and I returned to the table and told Mr. Xu that we would be happy to assist him. I directed that the shipment be consigned to Max. My responsibility would be to take care of the paperwork in the port when the shipment arrived. We also instructed Mr. Xu to see that the shipment was clearly labeled "personal effects."

A few days passed. We then received a message, via Jacqueline, that the shipment would arrive a few days later on the French freighter, SS Cambodge, and that it would be consigned to Max as we had directed.

While I exercised some broad oversight of the coolie stevedores and their employing company, I actually had no detailed knowledge of how the port system administratively functioned. I set about getting informed. I began by asking discrete questions in order to "gain a better understanding of my duties." I learned that goods consigned to Americans were processed by an American civil servant of the Defense Department who was positioned in the port offices. The person in that particular role was a Mr. Garner, who I then made a point of meeting. After a few conversations, we struck up a casual friendship. Mr. Garner was somewhat the common stereotype of a government clerk. He was overweight with a paunch and had reading glasses that hung on a cord around his neck. He wore a white short sleeved shirt that had a pocket protector holding several pens of different colors, and carried a pack of cigarettes in the other shirt pocket. To this attire was added a floppy straw hat, laying for the moment when I met with him, on the corner of his grey government-issued desk. Mr. Garner was chatty and amiable. He seemed a bit lonely and wanting company, and was more than happy to describe the import process to me in detail.

His explanation began: "When cargo arrives it is first determined if it is consigned to an American in Saigon on official duty, or consigned to an American military or governmental agency. Having been so segregated by the ship's staff, the accompanying bills of lading and manifest are delivered to Vietnamese clerks in the Port Captain's offices, together with the documents for the other commercial shipments," he explained. "If consigned to an American in Saigon in a duty capacity, the bill of lading so ratified by the clerks is forwarded to me," he added.

He continued, "I then check the various agency rosters for the individual in question and contact the person to advise that a shipment has arrived. After reviewing the bill of lading for the stated contents, and finding it reasonable, I stamp it as 'cleared' with an official seal that I keep here in my desk drawer. The individual in question then picks up the stamped bill of lading from me, at which point I check identification," said Mr. Garner. "Assuming everything is in order, the recipient then proceeds with the stamped bill of lading to the Vietnamese Customs shed, presents the document, and claims the shipment. An exception to this process is bulk shipments of military equipment. Those are usually consigned to the Vietnamese Army, but some are consigned to the Military Assistance Command for further control of distribution. Some large equipment shipments, for actual use by the U.S. Military, also follow a variation of the process," he said.

Since those kinds of military shipments were not relevant to what Max would be receiving for Mr. Xu, I did not bother to trouble Mr. Garner for expanded explanation. What I did note, however, was the drawer in which Mr. Garner kept the seal.

The following week, Max got a call from Mr. Garner that a cargo shipment in his name had arrived. Now familiar with the process, I had my driver, Loi, get a pickup truck, and collect Max. Then off we went to the port.

Arriving, I went directly to the desk of Mr. Garner, who recognized me from my prior visit. I introduced him to Max, who asked for the bill of lading in his name. Shuffling through a stack of papers, Mr. Garner produced a document of several pages on yellowed paper. Garner set about reviewing the document, while Max produced his ID card. Then Garner looked up, a bit surprised, and said "According to this bill of lading you are receiving a shipment of shoes, socks and plastic toys?" Although stunned, neither Max nor I showed any facial expression evidencing our shock. There was a long silence. Then I spoke up and said "Yes, we are assisting an orphanage project with a local church." Max quickly picked up the theme and said "We secured these products from a donor in Hong Kong."

Both of us remained calm and unflustered, smiling and showing no stress. Garner seemed satisfied, opened his desk drawer and stamped the bill of lading with the needed seal. Handing the document to Max, Garner added "Very generous of you young men to help the locals." Max and I left the port office without a word, joined Loi in the truck, and headed for the Customs shed. During the short ride, Max expressed his astonishment at the declared contents and remarked that we had clearly informed Mr Xu that it was to have been labeled "personal effects." I agreed, and complimented Max on his quick take up of my orphan story. We both thought we had safely emerged from a delicate circumstance and would soon be on our way.

Alas, that was not to be. Arriving at the Customs shed, we drove into the large, hangar-like building. We were directed into the center vehicle aisle where we were stopped by a uniformed Vietnamese Customs Officer. Upon Max presenting the sealed bill of lading, and his ID, we were informed that the shipment was among the large stock of recently arrived crates and would be brought to us. An assistant to the Customs Officer took a page from the document copies and scurried into a large maze of boxes and crates, followed by two coolies, from a larger group of coolies milling about. Several minutes passed and the assistant returned to the Customs Officer and muttered something, quietly, in Vietnamese. The Officer looked at the document, nodded, and the assistant left again, with four more coolies in tow. While not uttering a word, Max and I gave questioning looks to each other. Minutes later, the assistant returned again, followed by the six coolies towing a large flat wagon upon which rested a moderate sized crate about four feet in length, three feet wide and two to three feet deep. As they approached the Customs Officer, he moved to a low table structure at the side of the vehicle aisle, and called for the wagon and crate to be brought there. The coolies then took up two long steel poles, with wide leather straps connecting the two poles, one strap attached at each pole's end, but loosely such that the strap could slide up or down the poles. Four coolies, each holding one end of a pole, moved into position, two on either side of the wagon, lifting the poles such that the straps were loose and slightly beyond the crate at each end. Then two other two coolies slightly lifted and maneuvered the crate such that a leather strap was slid down the poles and tucked under each end of the crate. The crate then rested on the leather straps, one under each end, with two coolies on each side holding the poles. These four coolies then hoisted the poles on their shoulders such that the crate was suspended over the wagon bed.

The wagon was rolled forward, and they then carried the crate to the table structure near the Customs Officer. Positioning on each side of the table, they dropped the poles from their shoulders, and the crate came to rest, on top of the straps, on the table. Max and I observed that this was clearly a very, very heavy crate. The Customs Officer made the same observation and advised that in view of the contents being described on the bill of lading as "shoes, socks and plastic toys" the weight had drawn attention. He advised that the crate would need to be opened for inspection, the customs seal notwithstanding. With that, he directed a coolie to produce a crow bar and proceed to open the crate. The coolie began to peel off the nailed boards on the top of the crate, one at a time.

The coolies, the Customs Officer, his assistant– and Max and I – all stood watching to see what was inside. One board was peeled off, then another, and eventually all the ones on the top of the crate. There appeared a covering of brown cloth. A coolie slowly removed the cloth, tucked, as it was, into the sides of the crate, and we all saw a number of long tubes, wrapped in heavy brown paper, laid side-by-side, some four layers deep in the crate. They appeared to be about the length of a rifle. Max and I showed no emotion, but we both had visions of smuggled weapons. Thoughts of the Naval Prison in Portsmouth, New Hampshire crossed our minds! A coolie, at the direction of the Customs Officer, removed one of these wrapped items and carefully began to unroll the brown paper covering. We watched in intense anticipation. At the final roll off of the wrapped paper, a bolt of silk emerged!

Relief at it not being the worst of cases, we then had to quickly react as the Customs Officer looked to us with a quizzical expression and pointed to the bill of lading. Max, never missing a beat, stated in an indignant tone "Where are my shoes, socks and plastic toys!" I picked up the lead and followed with a similar expression of indignation "These are not our goods! Where are our shoes, socks and plastic toys?" The Customs Officer, at first defensive, slowly became skeptical. He advised us that claims of incorrect contents were not his concern, and that we needed to take it up with the French shipping company. In the meantime, we were told, the crate and bolts of silk would remain in the Customs shed. Max acknowledged his advice, and asked where we might find a senior official of the shipping line. We were directed to a modest building in the port complex and made our way there in our empty truck.

Entering, Max asked in his very fluent French, to see the official in charge, explaining to the reception clerk that it was about receipt of a shipment with incorrect contents. After about 10 minutes of waiting in the modest but comfortable reception area, we were escorted to the third (top) floor of the building and into a large and spacious office, with nearly wall-to-wall windows, allowing observation of the piers. There we were greeted by a tall Frenchman, dressed in a short sleeved khaki shirt, with epaulettes marked with some insignia, and khaki shorts. He advised that he was the senior officer of the French shipping company. Bearded, with salt-and-pepper grey hair, square jawed and with a tropical tan, he looked the very essence of the French Foreign Legion, of which he was likely a veteran.

His slight scowl showed that he expected a story of questionable truth. And he also showed a lack of any real interest as he sipped his tea under the ceiling fan, while gazing out the large window at the docks below.

Max eloquently spun our story of shoes, socks and plastic toys meant for an orphanage project - and our indignation at finding instead a crate filled with several dozen bolts of silk. Max asked sternly, "Where is our expected cargo and when will it be delivered?" The Frenchman listened politely, made a note or two on a pad on his desk, and said he would investigate it promptly. Yet he looked at us with clear skepticism, and some impatience.

He told Max that he would be contacted when the matter was resolved.

With that, he dismissed us.

As we turned to leave his office, it was clear that he had not believed a single word of what we had said.

The French are very worldly, and pragmatic.

Leaving the shipping company building, we had Loi immediately drive us to meet with Jacqueline at her apartment. Fortunately, she was at home. After Max described the events of the day to her, she said she would contact Mr. Xu, and get back to us with his advice on how to handle the matter as soon as possible. Max and I then headed for our house to decompress and assess the situation over a drink.

We both agreed that, so far, things had evolved as well as could be expected. We were concerned, however, about the longer term and final outcome. The crate remained in the Customs shed, filled with bolts of silk, and the bill of lading remained in the hands of the Customs Officer, with Max's name on it and an incorrect description of the contents. Thoughts of the Naval Prison again arose.

In the early evening, as Max and I were enjoying a glass of wine while awaiting Thi Ba's delicious dinner, Jacqueline appeared at the house. After accepting a glass of wine, she began: "I have contacted Mr Xu, and he is very disappointed with the situation. He said he would find a solution and you will be hearing from him soon." The three of us put the subject aside and enjoyed dinner and a quiet evening. The next day passed without further activity or communication. Then, late in the mid-morning of the following day, Jacqueline contacted Max at his office and conveyed the message that Mr. Xu had resolved the matter. She said to Max, "You and Jim are to meet Mr. Xu for lunch. At that time, he will instruct you as to next steps."

Max immediately contacted me. At high noon we met Mr. Xu at a small Chinese restaurant near our house in Cholon. Mr. Xu was known to be prompt and was already there. We chatted briefly, making polite small talk.

Then Max raised the subject at hand by asking "Why in the world was the crate labeled as 'shoes, socks and plastic toys?'" Mr. Xu asserted that he was as startled as were we, and that it was clearly an error at the shipping source. I added that it was now an even bigger risk for us should the military authorities have it brought to their attention by Vietnamese customs officials. Neither Max nor I raised the core issue of how these bolts of silk were supposedly "personal effects" as had been represented.

Mr. Xu then advised, "Since the goods are now in customs, and remained consigned to Max, you need to claim them again. However, there will be a new bill of lading, with another description of contents. You will be able to use it by following the same process as before." He instructed that we were to call for the bill of lading from a particular clerk in the offices of the Port Captain, secure the seal from Mr. Garner, and then proceed to claim the goods at the Customs shed, where, as Mr. Xu put it, there "would not be any problems." Although not stated, it was obvious that some consideration had been made to whatever parties in the resolution of the impasse.

Easy enough, it seemed, except for the part about Mr. Garner! Max and I were certain that if we showed up at his desk again within such a short period of time, it might raise some suspicion. And there was now the matter of a new bill of lading. We told Mr. Xu that we needed to think this one through. After some considerable discussion over dinner, Max and I concocted a plan. At first, we had considered abandoning the whole enterprise, but decided that would not serve as the crate and contents were in the Customs shed with Max's name on them. We considered the risk of where that might lead if the crate was not claimed.

So, following Mr. Xu's confident assertion that all was now arranged, we focused our attention on how to get the needed seal from Mr. Garner. The plan was for us to drop into his office, thank him for his prior assistance, and offer to take him to lunch as a way of becoming better acquainted. Certain that he was, as he seemed, somewhat lonely we expected that invitation would be readily accepted. The plan then called for us to leave the building for our car, where Loi was to drive us to a very nice café on the Rue Catinat. As we approached the car, I would suddenly say that I needed to return to the office and borrow a clerk's phone to make a very short call on a stevedoring matter. Max and Mr. Garner should just wait for a minute or two in the car.

I would then proceed directly to Garner's desk, documents discretely in hand, open his desk drawer, retrieve the seal, stamp the papers, return the seal to the drawer, and hurry back to the car. Should any of the Vietnamese clerks inquire, I would just say that Mr. Garner forgot something and I had come to get it for him.

The following morning, we set about executing our plan. Arriving at the port offices, Max first went to the Vietnamese clerks on duty and asked by name for the clerk who Mr. Xu had specified. I lingered in the doorway. The named clerk appeared and quickly handed Max the bill of lading documents without a word. I then approached Max as he left the counter and he passed me the documents, which I quickly tucked into a flat manila folder. We then both crossed the large open office area to the desk of Mr. Garner. He was not there! We walked back and asked another clerk if Mr. Garner was in the office and available. The clerk answered that he had been in all morning and perhaps had just stepped out for the washroom, or for a cup of tea from the small kitchen in the rear. Indeed, that soon became the case as we saw him returning to his desk. Max and I then approached him and followed through with the lunch invitation.

As expected, Mr. Garner readily accepted. The rest of the plan worked without flaw. I made my excuse as we were entering our car, returned to his desk, found the seal, stamped the documents (now in the manila folder I was carrying), hurried back to the car and we were off to lunch.

The lunch was pleasant enough, and we then dropped Mr. Garner back at the port. Loi then drove us to the motor pool and traded the sedan for a pickup. Now in the pickup with Loi at the wheel, we returned to the port and drove directly to the customs shed. The process was the same as before, being directed to the center vehicle lane and then stopped by the very same Customs Officer. He asked for the documents, which we handed to him for his scrutiny. He made no acknowledgment of ever having seen us before, glanced at the documents, and again ordered his assistant to take a copy and fetch the shipment. The assistant also gave no indication that he had ever seen us before, left with six coolies, and soon returned with the same crate on the same wagon. But this time there was a difference. The Customs Officer simply directed the crate to be lifted off and placed in the back of our pickup. Its weight was apparent as the coolies showed their exertion in lifting and moving it, and the bed of the pickup dropped a few inches when it was loaded. The Customs Officer then made a hand signal to the guards at the end of the vehicle lane where there was an exit from the Customs shed. Loi drove forward and we passed by the guards who gave us a friendly wave. In less than minute we were out of the port area and on the street, headed for a building in the central area of the city where Mr. Xu had given instruction to meet us.

Arriving there in about 20 minutes, we proceeded into an alley where there was a large open door leading into what looked to be a sizable storage room. Four coolies appeared and unloaded the crate, disappearing into the storage room. Mr. Xu then came out from the room, greeted us, and thanked us for our assistance.

No mention was made of his returning the favor. Max and I breathed a great sigh of relief. We decided to be much more cautious in doing favors for Jacqueline's friends in the future.

A curious cargo had been conveyed as a favor,
to be repaid.

CHAPTER
NINE

COLETTE

"It was both the most erotic and romantic experience of my life."

*I*t was mid-September, 1964, and Vietnam had risen to more attentive reporting in the U.S. press. Front page coverage reported South Vietnamese General Kahn publicly thanking younger officers under his command for successfully putting down an attempt by other Generals to displace him and the military triumvirate that had been ruling in recent weeks. General Kahn and General Minh, the titular senior member of the triumvirate, were reported to both be promptly visited by U.S. Ambassador Maxwell Taylor. The front page of the Times further reported U.S. leaders asking the Vietnamese to "put their disputes on ice" and to focus on "defeating the Reds" in a growing Viet Cong insurgency led by the North.

Notwithstanding such events, life in Saigon had continued largely unflustered. Following our misadventure with Mr. Xu, life did take another turn, however.

I finally found a romantic relationship.

Colette was French, or more correctly half-so. Her father was a French army officer and her mother a high-born Vietnamese.

This 5'4", petite, brown-eyed brunette had a marvelous figure, perfectly proportionate to her size. Like apparently all French women, Colette was charming and vivacious. Adding to her looks was her French accented English, which always stirred male attention. All this was supplemented by her gentle Vietnamese grace of motion which completed her bi-cultural character.

Colette and I first met at a party hosted by Jacqueline just a fortnight after my arrival in Saigon. The occasion was a farewell for Colette's imminent move to Paris. The cocktail gathering was in Jacqueline's apartment, located on a high floor with marvelous views of the river and city. When extending the invitation to Max and me, Jacqueline had assured us that besides enjoying the guests, we would also learn more about the city and Saigon life.

As a 22-year-old Navy Ensign new to Saigon, I was fascinated by the eclectic array of guests. Long forgotten is the fact that there were "UN Truce Observers" in those days before the real American war. The party attendance thus included Polish officers representing the Soviet bloc, Indians representing the neutral nations, and Canadians representing the Western allies. There were, as well, a few French officers still in the city; French and Vietnamese businessmen; the odd prosperous Chinese merchant; and American and European diplomats. Other guests included socialites from the city's upper class; a Catholic monsignor or two; a few American military officers, and, of course, Max and me. Exotic company indeed, for a young cowboy from Colorado!

In casual conversation with several of the guests, I learned that Colette was about to depart for Paris with her two-year-old daughter. Her reason for leaving Saigon was concern for the political environment. South Vietnamese President Diem and his brother had recently been assassinated. Things had become quite unstable.

I also learned from Jacqueline and other guests that Colette was 27 years old and recently divorced from a French Army doctor. They had three children. Her husband had taken their two young sons, ages six and four, with him to his new post in St Pierre et Michlon, off the east coast of Canada (the last remnant of French territory in North America). Colette had remained in Saigon with their daughter but now thought Paris a safer place, and was preparing to move there. She also had family there, from her father's side.

The evening progressed. I mostly enjoyed just people watching. This exotic group was all quite intriguing to me. I did engage in conversation with an Indian Army Signals Major, about sports. I also had a casual chat with a charming British woman, about local dining.

All the while I eyed Colette as she moved about the room, laughing, smiling, and making fleeting small talk with the guests. She exuded so much energy and charm as to cause her always to be in one's fascinated focus. Dancing began as the evening went on. It took place in the large parlor with a trio of Filipino musicians playing a mix of American and French music. The most played were the popular songs of Frank Sinatra and French singer Johnny Halladay. Colette was nearly always on the dance floor, each time with another guest. I couldn't help but notice that she commanded attention without even trying. It was just her charismatic nature.

All this I observed while leaning against the frame of an open balcony door, sipping a Negroni. I was transfixed at the sight of this striking young woman as she danced, mingled with guests, talked, and laughed. Her smile could have melted any man's heart; it was surely doing so to mine.

In time, she whisked past me, on her way to get another glass of wine. Then she stopped abruptly, turned to me, and said "I have been watching you and you have not danced!' Surprising even myself, I deftly replied, "I have been waiting to dance with you!"

With that, she took my hand and led me to the center of the floor. There, while shuffling about in a semblance of proper dancing, we conversed and I learned more about her. It largely confirmed what I had gathered earlier from others. But she now more quietly expressed her sadness at leaving the city she had known all her life. She acknowledged that she was familiar with Paris and had family there, but Saigon had been home. And while she looked forward, if cautiously, to a changed life style, she still had hesitation in leaving. She was clear, though, in her concerns about where matters seemed to be heading in Saigon, with regard to war.

The dance, our brief conversation, and for me the evening, all ended. She moved on in a cloud of perfume, chatter, and smiles. I took my leave quietly and departed.

Nearly five months passed. Max and I were long settled in the house in Cholon, and Max and Jacqueline had grown into a full-blown romantic relationship.

For my part, I was enjoying female company now and then. Some were younger Western women in the various diplomatic offices. Others were local friends of Jacqueline. Dinners with some, afternoon teas with others. But none "clicked" enough for me to pursue any romantic involvement. When in the company of Max and Jacqueline, I frequently mentioned my lingering fascination with Colette from the brief encounter at the party.

And then, late one afternoon, Jacqueline came by our house to inform me that Colette had returned to Saigon! She had found herself unhappy in Paris, it seemed, and decided not to live there after all. She was now a guest in Jacqueline's apartment until she found her own new lodging.

Jacqueline knew of my interest in Colette, and hence suggested that she bring her for dinner one evening. Of course, my enthusiastic answer was "yes" although my true sentiments were those of trepidation. I was anxious as to how I would get on with this sophisticated, older (for me), woman of such a vivacious nature.

Dinner I nevertheless set for the next day.

Wanting all to be perfect, I instructed Thi Ba to prepare her best French cuisine, select a compatible wine from our household stock, and prepare a special dessert. Thi Hai was instructed that our modest house was to be sparkling clean. And vases of fresh flowers were to be placed in the foyer, living and dining room areas.

I took great care in dressing for the evening. My choice was casual, with tasteful gray slacks and a white silk shirt. Both came from a tailor in Hong Kong which I had visited on my brief sea tour some months ago. Like a boy on his first date I was nervous. I was about to again encounter the most exciting woman I had ever met. She had not often left my mind from the moment I had first laid eyes on her five months ago.

Colette and Jacqueline arrived promptly at 7pm. I managed to maintain a quietly mature demeanor, yet warm, in hopes of exhibiting some sophistication and savoir faire. My hope was for Colette to see me as an eligible paramour rather than as a naïve young man five years her junior.

The evening began with cocktails and light hors d'ouvres prepared by Thi Ba. Conversation continued over dinner about Colette's time in Paris, world politics, and travel. Everything about the evening was delightful. Colette was attentive, even seeming interested in me. The ambiance was light and casual.

And then, with everything going beyond my expectations, a little after 10pm we heard the rumble of a motor vehicle engine just outside the house. A few moments later it was followed by a knock on the door. I left the table to answer the door and found a U.S. Army Military Policeman on the step, with another MP in the jeep close behind him. He smartly saluted and asked if this was the residence of two U.S. Navy officers. I answered in the affirmative, and the MP then advised me that he had been dispatched to contact us, as we had no phone at our registered quarters.

The message he delivered was that there had just been a Vietnamese military insurrection. The government had declared a curfew effective at 11pm. Anyone found on the streets after that hour was to be shot on sight. His instructions were that we were to remain in our quarters, side arms at hand. At 7am, when the overnight curfew was to be lifted, a driver would call for us and we were to report to our mobilization stations.

I thanked him, closed the door and returned to our dinner table with this startling news. Jacqueline was the first to offer practical comment. She said, "With an 11pm curfew, and it being now well after 10, there is no time for Colette and me to return to my apartment. We will have to stay until morning."

Since she and Max were now in an intimate relationship, this produced no awkwardness for them. After a brandy or two, and further conversation, they excused themselves to retire to Max's room.

That left me with Colette, another brandy, and forced conversation to avoid the inevitable subject of the sleeping arrangements. As midnight passed, and with the city eerily quiet, I finally broached the topic. "Colette," I said, "you might use my room and I will sleep on the sofa here in the living room."

With her musical laughter, she replied, "Don't be a silly boy, we will share your room."

I felt light beads of sweat forming on my brow. I was not at all certain what this meant or what to expect. My room had just one double bed. I felt a mix of anticipation... possibilities ...and boyish trepidation.

Colette and I finished our drinks and went quietly upstairs. She advised that the first thing she needed was some sleeping garb. Going straight to my armoir, she rifled through my hanging silk shirts and chose a light blue one, which she said would serve quite well. She then retired to the bath. Soon she returned wearing the silk shirt, covering her upper body. She had rolled the sleeves to fit the length of her arms. All that remained exposed were her beautiful legs. Now garbed in a night shirt of sensuous style, she further heightened my anxiety!

I then excused myself and went into the bath, undertook bedtime rituals of tooth brushing and washing, and donned gym suit pants. Returning to the bedroom I found Colette snuggled under the light covers, quiet, but awake.

The bed was sheathed with a mosquito net, and a ceiling fan stirred a very light draft. The bedroom had a balcony with high French doors that I left open to allow cool night air to enter. A full moon shining through the doors and the mosquito netting created a soft glow. Outside the city was silent, but in the distance, we could hear the low thunder of artillery cannon.

I climbed into the bed, staying carefully to one side. Neither of us spoke. I laid on my back, moon light glowing through the netting, cannons rumbling in the distance.

Then I heard Colette begin to cry, softly.

I turned to her, and saw tears falling on her cheek. I reached to catch one as it flowed. She took my hand, held it tightly, and said "I am so afraid."

I answered, "Don't be, I will protect you."

I gently kissed another tear slowing falling down her cheek. Then we both lay back, gently holding hands, spoke not another word, and soon fell asleep for the night. Those few hours were filled with a unique and profound emotional intimacy and sensual connection.

Over the coming weeks, I took to courting Colette. That first innocent night prefaced a learning experience. It began my first true love affair.

And it was, most certainly, both the most erotic and romantic experience of my life.

CHAPTER
TEN

BARTER

"To trade without using money" —WEBSTER

A I began my courtship of Colette, Max and I were also expanding our connections in Saigon. We befriended two Lieutenants who oversaw Clubs & Messes. Their duties included making various arrangements for visiting dignitaries as well as for entertainers in the USO events.

These Lieutenants often called on us for certain "special services." Aides to the generals also sought us out, as did some of the senior Naval officers. Over time the word had spread throughout the military community about our "special request" talents.

In addition to the Navy establishment, Max and I were often approached by Army and Air Force officers with such requests. With our roles in the motor pool, housing, Exchange, Commissary, SeaBee maintenance staff, and Port operations, there always seemed a need for some special service. We both were happy to assist nearly all comers. We kept track of the favors, as we expected them to be returned in time.

Shortly after starting my relationship with Colette, an Army Colonel approached me in my office. He was in command of a small squadron of "spotter planes" used to advise and assist the South Vietnamese Army. These planes were light, single engine Cessna two-seat aircraft used mostly for slow, low flights looking for Viet Cong units in the jungles. The pilots would then report their findings to the South Vietnamese for whatever combat action. The squadron was based at Ton Sun Nhut.

The Colonel, upon advice from unidentified sources, asked if I could assist him in securing some "Conex" cargo containers, which was the name attached to these steel shipping boxes. They were large containers used for shipping freight of various types, and were about 20' long, 9' wide and 8' high. Loaded aboard ships they could be stowed both below decks, as well as on deck, very efficiently; like building blocks. And they were valued for other uses, as well. In the rainy climate of Southeast Asia, the Conexes were used for many purposes. These included storage, small offices, and even field sleeping quarters. And they were very, very hard to come by!

A great many of these boxes could be found in the port, emptied out by stevedores after unloading them from commercial ships. They were then stored for reuse. As more goods entered the port than left, the stock of empty Conexes seemed to consistently grow. Despite the surplus of these boxes, they were not easily accessible. They were stored in a modestly controlled section of the port and monitored by the shipping companies. And, of course, moving them was a task of some consequential effort in itself.

The Colonel was anxious to secure two of these boxes. His needs: to provide secure parts storage on the flight line, and for a small line office on the airfield with shelter for the flight line crews in the regular monsoon rains. At the very time that I received this Colonel's request, I happened to be planning a romantic weekend with Colette to Cap St. Jacque. "The Cap" was located approximately 50 miles from Saigon, on the coast of the South China Sea. Colette was much connected to the town since she had been visiting there since she was a child. The small village seemed a transplant from the French Mediterranean coast. It was quaint and charming with small bed-and-breakfast pensions, sidewalk cafes, bars, and cozy restaurants. There were few, if any, motor vehicles in the community, and only one accommodation of size: The Hotel Pacifique.

Of all of the available village lodging, Colette favored one of the small pensions which had 12 beachfront suites, all facing the ocean and each with a small private patio. It was owned and operated by a genial, portly Frenchman. Each morning a French breakfast was available consisting of croissants and coffee, as well as fruit, boiled eggs and cold ham. Dinner was also served, and was at the choice of the owner/chef. The pension also offered a self-service honor bar. Each guest was asked to note their consumption in a small book on the bar counter. This was the first time I had encountered such an arrangement and my use was very cautious the first evening (I was to have my first after dinner Cherry Herring there in due course).

The guests were European. Most of them were French who traveled from Saigon to enjoy a weekend getaway. If one did not know better, you might have thought you were on the French Riviera. The challenge I had faced when contemplating our weekend getaway, however, was how to get to Cap St. Jacque. American military personnel were advised that leaving the city by ground transport was not only prohibited; it was exceptionally dangerous. There had been past incidents of Americans being kidnapped by Viet Cong within just a few kilometers of Saigon. And military personnel were at exceptional risk of being held captive or even being shot. The French, it seemed, were spared, as were the few other Europeans in the capital.

Colette was quite comfortable in driving her Citroen to Cap St. Jacque, as she had been doing for years. But I was not about to take that risk. Thus, there appeared an opportunity for barter in addressing the Colonel's request! After considering this now fortuitous matching of needs, I advised the Colonel that I would, indeed, get him two Conexes, and in short order. But the "trade" would be that one of his pilots fly me to Cap St. Jacque on Friday afternoon. A pilot would also pick me up late in the day on Sunday for return. The Colonel quickly, if curiously, agreed to the barter. We further agreed that I would have six such round-trip flights at my call, three for each Conex. The flights, of course, would be recorded as regular "spotting flights" or perhaps "training flights." That I left to him and the Army.

The first order of business was to deliver my end of the bargain. I proceeded promptly to scout the fenced-in, one-acre yard area in the port where the Conex stock was stored. Surprisingly there was little consequential security. The storage area had an open entry portal with two Vietnamese guards randomly patrolling the fenced yard. There were no check points as in the Customs area. It seemed easy enough to just pick up what I needed. My intended plan, then, was to show up at the fenced-in area, display an aura of authority, and just do it; although with some paperwork in hand – just in case.

My Army assistant, Ricky, prepared some vague requisition papers for Conexes left from military transport ships. The requisition stated that two Conexes were to be moved to the air base. To prepare for this transfer, I had my driver, Loi, select two other drivers in the motor pool squadron; ones who specialized in large trucks. Three days after meeting with the Colonel, I set about executing the plan. Loi and I arrived at the port. The drivers who Loi had chosen followed us, driving two "low boy" fourteen-wheeler trucks. After entering the open storage area, we got the attention of a coolie who was working a fork lift. After Loi spoke with him in Vietnamese, he followed us with his forklift to a stack of Conexes somewhat out of sight from the entry.

I had earlier scanned this cache of valuable steel boxes, choosing a spot with easy access for a wide vehicle. Loi directed the low boys to pull up near the containers. He then instructed the fork life operator to load one container on to each truck.

Forty-five minutes later the forklift operator had completed the task. I then pulled out a copy of the papers Ricky had prepared and handed it to the lift operator. Loi instructed him to show the paperwork to whomever might ask about our activities, IF anyone asked. With that, I handed a fistful of Vietnamese piasters to the fork lift operator before driving off. The low boys followed us, each with one Conex.

The next stop was the air base. Entering the base, of course, entailed some security inspection. After providing a copy of the requisition papers for review, we were allowed into the area with the low boys and the Conexes. Upon our arrival at the "Army sector" of the airfield, we were greeted by the Colonel. He had arranged a fork lift to unload the Conexes from the low boys, and directed that they be dropped in the squadron work area, adjacent to the airfield. Completing the delivery, I gave the low boy drivers a generous tip and sent them on their way. My end of the barter was now satisfied. That being the case, I felt comfortable asking the Colonel to arrange a flight to Cap St. Jacque for the weekend.

"Reservation confirmed" he amicably replied. As though the flight arrangements weren't enough, the Colonel then offered another benefit. He explained that there was an Army doctor, a Captain, posted in Cap St. Jacque, who lived in the Hotel Pacifique. The Colonel told me that the doctor had one of the half dozen U.S. motorized vehicles in Cap St. Jacque - an Army Jeep. He offered to arrange for the doctor to pick me up upon landing. I was delighted and took him up on him on his offer, rather than having Colette pick me up, with the associated complication of the timing of her arrival and accessing the airfield.

On Friday, I arrived at the air base and Loi dropped me off at the spotter plane operational area. The Colonel was waiting for me and minutes later saw me off on my 30-minute flight to Cap St. Jacque. We landed comfortably on a short runway, operated by the South Vietnamese Air Force. Upon landing, the Army doctor, notified by radio, was there waiting for me in his Jeep, as promised. He drove me to the pension where Colette had arranged our stay. Since she had not yet arrived, I checked in with the portly Frenchman. I then asked the doctor to join me for a late afternoon drink, which he accepted. As we enjoyed our gin and tonics, the doctor described his duties, which consisted of serving American advisors in this region. While most were Army infantry officers, he said there was one Navy lieutenant who worked with the South Vietnamese coastal forces. The doctor went on to explain that most of the medical attention focused on stomach ailments, fevers, and flesh infections deriving from the jungle environment. Serious injury called for helicopter medevac flights to Saigon, and was infrequent.

Colette arrived in due course, her drive uneventful. I invited the doctor to join us for dinner, which he accepted. He knew the French pension host, as well as apparently everyone else in town. His own French was quite good, which charmed Colette. She reminisced about her many earlier visits to the town, starting from her childhood. During dinner, the doctor told me that the Colonel had informed him as to how my traveling by spotter plane had come about. That expanded the conversation to what he described as an "equipment need." Compared to the Colonel's request, the doctor's request was a simple one: he needed some picnic coolers! He explained that these coolers would come in handy when traveling in the region with medications that needed to stay chilled.

Since this was such a simple need, I asked the doctor if he had tried to get them through Army channels. He said that he had, but to no avail. He told me that he was certain that the Quartermaster depot in Saigon did have coolers. But his official requisitions had been rebuffed, without explanation. I informed him that I was not aware of any such product in the Navy inventory but would check it upon returning to Saigon, on the following Monday. I also suggested that he advise the Colonel that if I were successful in getting him a few coolers, it would warrant another weekend round trip flight! Upon my Sunday return to Saigon, and then to my office on Monday, I asked Ricky to research the "cooler project." He first confirmed that there were none in Navy stock. He had found, however, that the Army did have coolers. Ricky also learned that they were earmarked for only "welfare and recreational use." (As if anyone was going to go picnicking in the jungle!)

The next challenge, then, was to get our hands on the Army stock. Ricky suggested an "inter-service" requisition as the process. After complimenting him for his creative solution, I asked him to do just that – prepare a requisition for two large coolers. With admirable creativity, Ricky prepared the necessary paperwork. I instructed him to have the requisition describe that these items were needed for certain "classified naval operations."

With requisition in hand, Loi drove me to the Quartermaster facility and to the warehouse where these coolers were housed. After an Army corporal greeted me, I presented him with the requisition. Scrutinizing it, he remarked, "There is an error here. An inter-service requisition has 10 digits; this one has only nine." I asked to review the document and, of course, agreed with his observation. "May I use your phone," I asked. "There appears to be a typo. I will call my Army assistant to get the correct number." The corporal nodded and directed me to a desk with a phone on it. I called Ricky, but there was no answer. Thinking quickly, I deftly pushed down the button on the receiver cradle, effectively hanging up. Holding the button down, I kept talking as though my Army assistant were on the other end of the line.

"The requisition number is a digit short. Did you make an error?" (Pause)

"Then read me the full number." (Pause)

"OK, it looks like you dropped the last digit. I will write it on this copy. Correct your file copy." (Pause)

"Thanks, and the next time, let's be more careful!"

At that, I truly hung up the phone and wrote the number "three" on the requisition form as the missing last digit.

After again reviewing the document, the Army Corporal now found the inter-service requisition form to be satisfactory. With Loi's help, he transferred the two coolers from the warehouse area to the trunk and back seat of my car. Before we sped off, I cordially thanked him for his service.

The following Friday, I was off to Cap St. Jacque once again - - with coolers in tow. And, once again, the doctor met me with his Jeep. He was both thrilled and impressed with the timely service. He also confirmed my additional flight services, compliments of the Colonel.

For a few months thereafter, I essentially had my own private air service. And no one ever did inquire about the source of the Conexes, or the coolers. Whatever became of the inter-service paperwork remains a military mystery.

The spirit haunting our Cholon house, however, did not seem open to barter, or bargaining.

Barter had proven, at least for the moment,
quite effective.

CHAPTER
ELEVEN
HAUNTED

"Haunt: to appear as a spirit" —WEBSTER

knew the house was haunted when we moved in. Jacqueline had warned us, explaining that this was the very reason that the rent was so reasonable. As Westerners, however, it was expected that we would ignore the warning.

And we did.

The neighborhood scuttlebutt was that decades ago there had been a murder in the house. As the story had it, the woman who had been killed now haunted the place as a way of seeking solace, or revenge. While this was readily accepted among the neighboring Chinese, Max and I considered it to be nothing more than local folklore.

During the first few weeks that we lived in the house, there was no evidence of occupying spirits. During our third month, however, an incident occurred. One evening we observed our house dog, Gitan, trying to dig into the living room tile floor. She kept growling furiously and scraping the floor with her paws. It was as though she were trying to uncover whatever had sparked her senses. The servants tried to calm

Gitan, to no avail. After several minutes, Thi Ba picked up Gitan and took her into the kitchen. Moving the dog to another room, however, did not have the calming effect she had hoped. Instead, Gitan continued to growl and scratched at the kitchen door in trying to return to the living room. After nearly an hour, the dog finally settled down.

Max and I found the whole matter curious. We asked Thi Ba and Thi Hai what in the world was wrong with their dog. We asked them if the reason for its behavior was perhaps a food odor on the living room floor, or perhaps a cat or rodent had found its way into the house and urinated on that spot. Thi Ba very matter-of-factly replied, "No, it was the spirit." Max and I, of course, certainly did not believe Thi Ba, but rather than offending her by directly contradicting her superstitions, we simply dropped the subject.

A week later, another strange "happening" occurred. Max and I were sitting in the living room reading and sipping our after-dinner drinks. We each looked up from our books after hearing the sound of footsteps in the foyer. We knew that these footsteps could not have been Thi Ba or Thi Hai since they both moved around the house barefoot. Then after a few minutes, the sound of these footsteps stopped. We both shrugged off this incident and went back to reading and enjoying our brandies. The following week, the occurrence of unusual sounds reached a new level. During the middle of the night, Max and I were both awakened to what seemed like someone softly banging pots and pans in the kitchen. He and I walked out of our bedrooms at the same time and headed to the staircase landing. At that point, we again heard the sound of footsteps in the foyer. Moments later, both Thi Ba and Thi Hai walked into the foyer from their bedrooms located off the kitchen. We could tell from their faces that they were quite frightened. After seeing Max and me on the stair case landing above, they frantically cried, "It is the spirit!"

Max and I hurried down the stairs to comfort them, offering other explanations for the noise. Perhaps from rodents in the kitchen cupboards knocking over pans, or Gitan chasing a mouse? We assured them that we would call an exterminator first thing in the morning to place traps around the house.

As for the sound of the footsteps, we tried to dismiss them by saying that the night breeze could have caused a door to swing and bang about. But we could tell from their still frightened expressions that neither Thi Ba nor Thi Hai accepted our explanations. They had calmed down enough, though, to return to their bedrooms holding hands in comforting each other.

During the next few weeks, still more incidents occurred. Max and I were out one evening, and the minute we returned, Thi Ba and Thi Hai reported that they had seen the spirit! They described it as a female figure, clothed in a long dress and cloak, with a shawl covering its head. While footsteps could clearly be heard, the figure was actually floating several inches above the ground; and no feet were seen. The spirit also kept its head turned in such a way that its face was not seen either.

In addition to this spirit sighting, Gitan continued to dig, in an agitated fashion, over the spot on the tiled living room floor several times a week. Each time her actions were more frenzied.

As though the sighting and Gitan's actions were not unsettling enough, we occasionally heard more odd sounds during the middle of the night. Sometimes it sounded like someone was banging a pan; other times we heard a soft whimper or crying.

It was now October, with Halloween approaching. That seemed to spark our interest in the occult, and more interest in our haunted house. As for Vietnam, the press at home was gaining more interest, as well. The Times now featured front page news such as the North Vietnamese claiming that U.S. and South Vietnamese forces had shelled the southern-most province of the North; but that front page column was shared with larger news type columns reporting on the Vatican, a Rhodesian threat to break ties with Great Britain, and coverage of the forthcoming election.

As for our matter, after living in the house for almost six months, an incident finally occurred that convinced both Max and me that the house might, indeed, be haunted!

It was around 11pm and Max and I had retired for the evening to our respective bedrooms. We had done so at separate times, not too many minutes apart. Suddenly, we both heard the sound of footsteps, but this time the footsteps were heard on the marble stairs leading to the second floor. Without a doubt, we heard slow, measured footsteps as one would expect from someone slowly climbing stairs.

We both knew that it could not be either of the servants since they moved about barefoot. And since both Max and I were in the habit of leaving our shoes each night at the foot of the staircase, for Thi Hai to polish, we each knew that it was not the sound of the other.

The only conclusion we each could draw was that we had an intruder in the house! Both Max and I appeared on the stair landing within seconds of one another. No one was there. The house was quiet. Neither the dog nor the servants appeared to have heard the sound that Max and I had heard. The only thing that we both knew for certain is that we had definitely heard measured footsteps on the marble stairs that lead to the second floor.

With our adrenaline flowing, Max and I talked for several minutes in search of an explanation. Finding none, we each went back to our bedrooms. After nearly an hour, I finally dozed off.

The following morning, Max asked Thi Ba and Thi Hai if they had heard any strange sounds the night before. They said that they had heard nothing. He told them what we had heard. They suggested, in reply, that the spirit was wishing to make its presence known to us, as the "masters of the house."

Then, several days later, Thi Ba and Thi Hai saw the spirit once again. Like before, it wore a long dress, cloak and shawl. Neither its face nor its feet was apparent. The only sound heard was its footsteps. The night following this report, Max and I had another personal experience. Again, after both of us retired to our bedrooms, we heard a noise. This time it was the metal accordion security gate to the third-floor roof terrace. The gate was located inside the locked wooden door. The sound we heard was an intermittent squeak, as if the locked security gate was being slowly opened. Both of us bolted from our rooms at the same instant with pistols in hand. We were certain someone was breaking in. Turning on the stairwell light and staying near the wall, we prepared to move up the staircase. And then we saw – nothing! After checking the security gate and the wooden door, to find both soundly locked, we roused the servants. The four of us set about doing a thorough search of the house. Nothing. And throughout our hunt, Gitan remained perfectly quiet.

Thi Ba and Thi Hai then insisted that the spirit was sending us a message. They told us that we needed to be very cautious and "offer it the highest respect." As a way of comforting them, we assured them that we would take their advice and that first thing the following morning, we would consult with Jacqueline. As promised, we reached out to Jacqueline late the following morning only to learn that she was in Hong Kong and would return to Saigon any day.

For a few days, things were quiet. Then one morning I awoke with a serious fever. Registering 102 degrees on the thermometer we kept in our household first aid kit, Max insisted that we head for the Naval hospital. Loi drove us there. Max accompanied me and, as the good friend he was, stayed with me for a few hours until I was finally settled. After the Navy doctor conducted a thorough examination, he advised that it was an "undiagnosed fever," and had me admitted. I was now in a hospital bed.

The Navy corpsman on duty connected me with intravenous needles attached to bags for both hydration and to lower the fever with antibiotics. At that point, I was weak and groggy. Max departed, promising me that he would be back to visit the following morning. It just so happened that Jacqueline returned the same afternoon that I was admitted. Max met with her to update her on what had transpired during the past few days. What was of utmost importance to us was for Jacqueline to help calm down the servants who had now become quite frantic at my falling ill. Meanwhile, I remained hospitalized and the doctors still could not figure out the cause of the fever, which was steady at 101 degrees!

During my second day in the hospital, my fever had not improved. My temperature continued to fluctuate between 100 and 102 degrees. There was no clear diagnosis. I drifted in and out of a restless sleep. Then during the second night of my hospitalization, around 1:00 am, I awoke. I felt weak but could clearly feel that I was no longer feverish. I buzzed for a corpsman, who came promptly and checked my temperature. He confirmed that it had returned to 98.6 degrees. At about 6am that morning, the Navy doctor came to see me during his morning rounds. Briefed by the corpsman of my fever abatement, he saw me first. He checked the temperature again and remarked that the fever had disappeared as mysteriously as it had arrived. He prescribed that I stay another 48 hours to confirm that it was gone. He also wanted to ensure that I was fully hydrated before being discharged.

About 9:00 am, Max arrived to check on me. I shared the good news of the fever breaking and my pending release after two more days. Max gasped, blanched, and was clearly startled. He asked me to repeat the time when this had occurred. I stated about 1:00 am that morning. Max then told me his story of the previous evening.

Jacqueline had joined him for dinner at the house. After dinner, the servants had a long discussion with her, and then announced to Max that they were certain that I would soon die as the result of the spirt striking me with the fever. And to prevent that, they insisted on setting up a small altar in my room with flowers, joss sticks, fruit, rice, and candles.

These were to be offerings to the spirit, and Max himself needed to participate. Prayers and petitions would be offered. If he refused, they were then going to leave our employment immediately as they wanted no part in my death.

Jacqueline counseled Max to agree to participate in the ceremony. She told him that he must also do so with a serious demeanor. He agreed, over fear of losing our two excellent servants!

Thi Ba and Thi Hai set the hour of the offering as midnight. Promptly at the appointed hour, the four of them gathered in my room. They made a small altar of an end table, and on it placed a white cloth covering, then flowers, fruit, rice, joss sticks, and candles. Then the servants undertook some chants and prayers in Vietnamese. Jacqueline added her own. And Max muttered a few Hail Mary's in French. The peculiar ceremony lasted about 40 minutes. The candles were left to burn down, as were the joss sticks.

Needless to say, both Max and I were astonished at the coincidence of timing between this ad hoc ritual and the breaking of my fever.

We decided to move!
It seemed a spirit had, indeed, appeared.

CHAPTER
TWELVE
UP-GRADE

"To raise to a higher standard" — WEBSTER

After the mysterious experience with the spirit, Max and I were quite committed to moving. In fact, we had already been considering the prospect for a few weeks, but for quite different reasons. Our social circle and connections had been expanding rapidly, and along with them our entertaining habits. The Cholon house was now thought to be a detriment to our improving hospitality. It was in a dense, somewhat crowded neighborhood, and not the easiest to locate. The favored upper-end residential areas of the city, by contrast, offered tree lined streets, more distance between houses, and lawns and gardens. The houses in those areas had a clearly French character, from architecture to decor. In general, those sectors were much like comparable neighborhoods in Paris, as one might expect after a century of French occupation and French dominance of the urban culture.

Our finances had been improving. With evolving political uncertainty, and increasing conflict with the North, the piaster value of the dollar had been rising regularly. Combined with our bartering skills, the improved currency conversion with the Indian booksellers suggested that we could now afford more comfortable lodging. The experience with "the spirit" just served to prompt us to action. We chose to have Colette guide our choice. Upon return to Saigon, she had taken a small bungalow at 232b Rue Pasteur, near the Cathedral. A modest, very quaint house, set behind a much larger one of 19th century stock. It was accessed by a lengthy drive on the side of the primary residence, and quite comfortable. This was an excellent neighborhood where nearly all the American Generals, Captain K, and the senior diplomats lived. And, of course, this sector was also home to the Vietnamese gentry and prosperous Europeans in residence in the city.

In just a few days, Colette found what seemed to be the perfect place, quite near her own abode. It was a moderately sized two-story wooden house, with three bedrooms. Located in the Rue Croix Rouge, across from the French Embassy. It was clearly an address of distinction. The main floor had a comfortably large living/entertaining area, a dining room that could seat 10 easily, a very modern kitchen, and servant's quarters to the rear. The bedrooms were on the second floor, all three comfortably sized, and a large shared bath. The yard area was modest, but offered ample green space with some flower beds, and a sense of privacy. There was a small porch on the front, which added some distinction to the house, and with flower boxes added color, as well. The tree lined street provided both charm and shade.

We took it!

Although our finances had improved, we decided to add another roommate to mitigate the increased cost. To that end, we asked a fellow officer with whom I served in the port to join us. He was an ROTC graduate of Northwestern and had arrived in Saigon a few months before Max and me. He was very quiet and thoughtful, with a charming and delightful personality that we were certain would blend with our social circle. We were all three Ensigns, commissioned in June 1963, and thus of comparable rank. And while Max and I had cars and drivers, our new resident came with a motorcycle!

As we made the move, with a load of still newer Navy furniture, we introduced our new housemate to Thi Ba and Thi Hai. They had taken to calling Max and me "Monsieur Max" and "Monsieur Jim" respectively. With now another "Jim" in the household, they dubbed him "Monsieur Moto," in consideration of his motorcycle.

Within just a few days we were fully settled and the good life continued - and expanded. In our frequent entertainments, we had become known as the only Ensigns in the Far East who would invite Generals to dinner – and they would come! Capitan K lived just a few blocks from us, and we became regular guests at his social gatherings, as well. Jacqueline and Colette added to our growing social network as they frequently brought guests for dinner. They most often had us include two of their beautiful lady friends to balance the dinner table, as our guests were often single officers. Their friends were Mimi Fogt and Jacqueline Carouseux, "Jackie C" as we came to call her. Both were French-Vietnamese, well educated, in their late 20s. Word of these new, frequent dinner guests also enhanced the acceptance of our invitations among our bachelor American diplomatic and military officer friends.

Fully re-settled in a fortnight, we resumed our comfortable and active life. We christened the new dining room with a dinner for ten. Two of the guests were the Lieutenants who ran the Officer's clubs, Larry and Glenn by name. They were senior to us by 4 years, single, and delighted to join us with Mimi and Jackie C as dinner companions. Larry was Naval Academy Class of '59 and Glenn an ROTC officer from Princeton in the same year group. A junior CIA officer was also invited, who came with a strikingly beautiful Taiwanese named Janney Sun. Monsieur Moto had duty that evening.

The house and the neighborhood seemed to infect our gatherings with a new sense of more elegant ambiance. The French dinner prepared by Thi Ba was excellent, as usual. The conversation diverse and sparkling, with the expected flirtations among the dinner pairings. Among other topics, we discussed the current state of nightlife in Saigon. It was beginning to take on a bit of an American flavor, although still dominantly French. The nightspot of choice remained the Moulin Rouge. Dark, with lots of red velvet, small tables with candle lighting, telephones at each table, tuxedo attired waiters and a multi-lingual maitre'de. Pricey by the standards of the day, but worth it for the Parisian charm and quality of the singers and musicians.

A current songstress of note was Bach Yen. A very lovely young Vietnamese, who sang marvelously in both French and English. Larry had encountered her at some point, and referenced a developing personal friendship if not a romantic attachment. There was some discussion as to whether Vietnamese entertainers might soon find favorable audiences in the U.S. since Vietnam itself was getting heightened attention in the American press.

And, though earnestly smitten with Colette, I could not help but be attracted to the striking Janney Sun. She had some sort of position in the Taiwanese Embassy, and seemed purposely vague about her role. Given that her date for the evening was our CIA friend, we assumed it was something to do with intelligence matters.

In any event, both she and Bach Yen were soon to have a role in our further adventures.

Both residence and adventure seemed
to now be up-graded.

CHAPTER
THIRTEEN
BACH YEN

"Song softens the mind more than sermons." — NAPOLEON

And song can soften the heart, as well. Or so thought Larry and Glenn. They were nearing the end of their tour in Saigon when Max and I met them. Their acquaintance came about through our efforts to buy their Citroen, which they drove during their time in Saigon. Max and I had considered acquiring this high-performance sedan as it was quite regal in style. Black with rear doors that opened broadly from a rear hinge. Seen frequently in films, it was an auto that smacked of 1930's Europe and was very French!

We thought it would add a bit of panache to our own style.

The softening of hearts was what prompted Larry and Glenn's decision to undertake sponsoring Bach Yen, a young Vietnamese singer. They were attempting to send her to the U.S. for a TV appearance so that the American public could have a closer view of the Vietnamese people. The hope was that it would ease some of the emerging tension at home in the ever-growing American involvement in the conflict between North and South Vietnam. Bach Yen was 19 years old at the time and had been singing professionally for some years. As a teenager, she had gone to Paris in 1961 and appeared in various venues. She also had recorded a few albums before returning to Saigon.

Max and I learned about Larry and Glenn's intended professional involvement with Bach Yen one evening during a dinner at our house on the Rue Croix Rouge. For some time, Glenn had been pursuing the prospect of having Bach Yen make an appearance on the Ed Sullivan show. That show was, at the time, the premier variety television program shown nationally in the U.S. on Sunday evenings. Larry, for his part, had been working the U.S. Embassy in Saigon for the needed visas for both Bach Yen and her mother (who insisted that she accompany her daughter during any trip abroad).

Neither Larry nor Glenn had yet addressed the costs of travel and lodging. Although they both were about to be transferred back to the U.S., the details of their grand plan were far from resolved.

Familiar with our "fix it" reputations, they asked if we could help. Indeed, we could.

Our dinner conversation turned to devising a plan.

The plan called for a number of tasks. Glenn, upon being discharged from active duty, would proceed to New York to lock in an appearance for Bach Yen on The Ed Sullivan Show. He would also search out complimentary lodging in New York.

Larry was also leaving active service and moving to Los Angeles. His mission would be to find an airline to donate travel for Bach Yen and her mother.

Max would work with the local office of the U.S. Information Agency (USIA) to get them to record and film Bach Yen during a local performance. The film would be used to assist with the booking on Ed Sullivan, and in securing donated lodging and travel.

And I would work on the needed U.S. visas through our Embassy contacts.

A few weeks later, Larry and Glenn departed for the U.S. and began their assigned tasks. Max and I remained in Saigon and quickly took to our assignments. Having done some "favors" for various members of the Embassy staff, these did not prove too difficult to fulfill. Max was able to arrange a USIA filming and recording of Bach Yen, which we promptly shipped to Glenn in New York to assist his pursuit of the booking on the Ed Sullivan show. Another went to Larry for similar use in securing transportation. I used Embassy contacts derived from "favors" and was making swift progress with the needed visas for Bach Yen and her mother.

But we did encounter one unforeseen obstacle. Unbeknownst to us, Bach Yen and her mother also needed permission from the South Vietnamese government to travel to the U.S. and Europe (an "exit visa" of sorts). And that was a pre-condition to issuance of the U.S. visa for entry. The Vietnamese government was proving to be stridently bureaucratic. It did not offer even a guesstimate of the length of time in which these exit visas could be issued. Unfortunately, Max and I were not quite so well connected with Vietnamese government people as we were with our own.

We then recalled Mr. Xu and his seemingly magical resolution of the Customs matter involving our shipment of shoes, socks, and plastic toys. And we remembered that he owed us a favor!

We contacted Jacqueline and shared our predicament with her. She then spoke with Mr. Xu, who replied promptly to Jacqueline telling her what it would take to easily resolve the dilemma. That, it turned out, amounted to simply securing a modest amount of specified American hard liquor, together with a courtesy evening for four at Bach Yen's show at the Dai Kim Do club. Voila! The exit visa matter was quickly resolved.

Glenn also experienced success with the Ed Sullivan staff. Bach Yen was booked for a January, 1965 appearance. Larry also was making transportation progress, and in time TWA committed to courtesy transport to New York. After two more weeks we secured the visas allowing Bach Yen and her mother to depart for New York, just after Christmas. And the timing seemed now quite propitious as news of Vietnam was elevating in the U.S. press. The Times headlined U.S. planes attacking a bridge in the north, and President Johnson's request of Congress for added foreign aid and military assistance to South Vietnam.

The January appearance on the show proved a big success! The four of us had visions of becoming successful producers and talent agents!

In fact, Bach Yen and her mother did stay in the U.S. for 12 years. Bach Yen started with Larry as her manager, who sought out small venues around the country. Only marginally successful with Larry, she ended the relationship with our group, and contracted with a professional talent firm in Los Angeles. She took to more extended travel, performing in small clubs and in quality hotels. She also landed a role in the John Wayne movie "The Green Berets," and even recorded the soundtrack.

Glenn and Larry went about their civilian lives.

Max and I, however, had one more adventure that involved Bach Yen. This occurred on Christmas Eve 1964, just before she left Saigon.

Oh, and we never did buy the Citroen.

Her song had certainly softened our hearts.

CHAPTER
FOURTEEN
PROMOTION

*"What might be hoped, if each who behaved well had a chance at becoming a General one day." —*NAPOLEON

Napoleon never did pay much attention to his Navy, but the phrase applies, as well, to the sea service and the prospects of becoming an Admiral. Not that Max and I were necessarily behaving well. Promotion nonetheless loomed on the horizon for us and our new housemate, "Monsieur Moto." In the day, a promotion to Lieutenant Junior Grade (a "jg") was nearly automatic after eighteen months of service. Early December was the anticipated date to add a half stripe to our uniforms and shoulder boards.

The custom in the naval service was that one was expected to entertain one's fellow officers on such occasions. The cultural term was to host a "wetting down party" so as to "wet down" your new stripe with ample drink. A good party called for good planning and we set about preparations in September, nearly three months in advance of the date. The first order of business was selection of a venue. Colette recommended a moderately upscale bar on the Boulevard Charner, where we could largely buy out the house for a few hours in the early evening. Other suggestions were also forthcoming from Jacqueline.

While considering the venue options, however, we quickly concluded that the choice would be driven by the number of guests. So, we deferred venue selection to instead focus on our guest list. Of course, the first guests to come to mind were all the Navy officers in the city. We were quickly able to secure the HEDSUPACT list from Captain K's yeoman. To that we added those at the Naval Hospital, a few attached to Army and Air Force units, as well as the few Navy officers on Joint Staffs.

Then another consideration emerged. The senior grade Navy officers also had their families in residence, and as we anticipated including Colette and Jacqueline in the evening, it seemed appropriate to include the wives of those officers. It was emerging nonetheless as a male dominated gathering. We then considered our now very warm relationships with the wives of the Generals, fostered through our Sector Warden duties. So, we decided, we would invite all the Generals and their wives. That would add more female participation, and would certainly add to the glamor of the evening.

Then still another consideration come to the fore. With the dominance of Navy officer guests, the Generals might feel out of place in what was, after all, a gathering in a Navy tradition. How to make them feel comfortable? The answer was to invite all the Army and Air Force officers on each of the General's immediate staffs – with wives where that applied.

Once again, using our well-developed connections, we obtained the lists of all those officers. The full guest count now approached 300.

With such a prospectively large gathering, the various bar venues under consideration were inadequate. We pondered the matter briefly, and then agreed that THE most prominent place in the city was the Hotel Caravelle! It offered large gathering spaces, was centrally located, and was also a venue where any security issues could be more easily addressed. We set about making the arrangements for what was soon to be a spectacular and newsworthy event. The Caravelle was relatively new, having opened to the public at Christmas in 1959. It offered extensive Italian marble, bullet proof glass and state of the art air conditioning. Of modern design, the 10th floor offered a roof top ball room, with a surrounding exterior balcony. It also housed the Saigon news bureaus of NBC, CBS and ABC. The press reporters regularly gathered in the bar on the 9th floor. In August, not long after the Gulf of Tonkin naval incident, there had been a bombing at the Caravelle. It was in a room on the 5th floor, a floor mostly occupied by the journalists. Fortunately, there were no fatalities among the nine rooms damaged, but some injuries, largely from glass blown out of the windows and showering on the street below. The beneficial result was greatly enhanced hotel security, which very much suited our needs!

Max and I called on the General Manager of the Caravelle, a Frenchman by the name of Andre de Lapine. Elegant, and surprisingly neither overly formal nor officious, he welcomed us to his office for a pre-arranged meeting. We advised of the festive date, December 5th, and the expected number of guests. (He assisted with that count by offering a suggestion on the likely percentage of acceptances from among those invited.) He also toured us through the hotel and the choice of spaces.

Given the large number of expected guests, we all agreed that the roof top ball room was really the only spot that suited. In addition to the ample open space and dance floor, the outside balcony on three sides of the building allowed overflow, or just a break for fresh air and a gaze at the stars. We then turned our attention to a theme. What resulted was a sea setting aboard the "USS Jay Gee." I arranged for the SeaBees to construct a modest mast and cross bar, complete with lines and a base allowing it to be placed on the floor. It was to be festooned with a few Navy pennants. We asked Andre to provide a podium covered completely with blue cloth, trimmed with gold ribbon, on which would be a guest book to "log in." This entry was to be "manned" by two enlisted sailors in their dress whites, one on either side of the podium, who would dutifully salute each guest as they signed in.

Andre became quite fascinated with our creative ideas and asked for whom the party was being held. Given our youth, he not surprisingly assumed it was for some senior officer. We advised that it was OUR party, for our promotion. He was both startled and delighted. Now caught up in the spirit of the event, he offered to have alternate blue and gold silk curtains hung ceiling-to-floor around the ballroom. And he also offered a blue and gold rug to place in front of the podium. In time, added details included a full array of Navy signal flags hung around the ballroom, and blue and gold balloons at various heights.

This new sponsorship information, for Andre, also provoked the question of payment. We had already made a substantial deposit, and after some discussion concluded that we could handle the balance with both cash and the prospect of "favors" as Andre might find helpful. As for refreshments, there were to be two bars providing a wide variety of drinks, a dozen tables in various locations with mixed hors d'ouvres, and 4 waiters constantly patrolling the room with offerings of candy, cigars, and cigarettes from silver trays. On either end of the room would be a "champagne fountain." Topping off the arrangements would be a nine-piece stringed orchestra, offering French and American selections.

All this was worked out with Andre over a few weeks, allowing ample lead time for the many special preparations. Meanwhile we separately arranged for printed invitations while editing the guest list. Some 240 guests were eventually invited, about 4 weeks before the event, and 194 accepted. These included nine Generals, most prominent among them being General Westmoreland.

Just ten days before the party, the astute Army assistant in my office, Ricky, reminded me that any gathering of more than 25 Americans required notification to the Provost Marshal in the Military Police office. This was in order to arrange appropriate security, if deemed necessary. Thus reminded, I promptly called personally on the Provost's office in the Army headquarters.

Upon arrival I advised the clerk of my purpose in calling, and was presented with a form to complete. Questions to be answered were date and place, number of guests, hours, purpose of the gathering and the like. I dutifully completed the form, returned it to the clerk, who in turn passed it a Sergeant sitting at a desk. I observed the Sergeant reviewing the form. He looked up and called for me to approach his desk behind the counter. Now seated opposite him at his desk, he asked for some clarifications. What was a "wetting down" party? Had we made any private security arrangements? Were there any General officers expected to attend?

The Sergeant moved very quickly past that last question, seeming about to check the "no" box on his form, when I replied "yes." Clearly startled at the reply, he looked up hastily and asked "Did you say 'yes'.....'yes', as to General officer's attending?"

I confirmed that I had, indeed, so answered.

"How many?" he then asked, looking at me directly.

"Twelve invited but it appears only nine will attend," I replied.

Standing up abruptly, the Sergeant said, "Wait here. I need to speak with the Major."

With that he went into an office with glass windows, behind which I could see an Army Major at his desk. The two began to converse while reviewing the form, with much head nodding. Then both turned to look at me waiting at the Sergeant's desk. The Major motioned for me to come into the office. I entered, saluted the Major as my senior, and stood at attention. He put me "at ease" and began to ask for more details about the party. I then asked if he was not already aware of the event? He answered in the negative, and I quickly offered an apology that he had apparently not been invited. Confused at my comment, he asked why he would have been invited. I explained our rationale of inviting the more senior Army officers so as to make the Generals comfortable. I also suggested that our list must have been incomplete as he would certainly have appeared on it as the Provost. To that he replied that he had just reported in about two weeks ago. That, I offered, explained the oversight. I told him an invitation would be forthcoming before the end of the day.

Then we returned to discussing security needs in view of the several senior officers to be in attendance. The Major assured me that all would be in order for the event, and that he would deal directly with the hotel security staff and the Vietnamese police. He closed his comments with assurance that he would also attend the party!

December 5th came upon us quickly. Security for the evening called for the public square in front of the hotel to be completely blocked with barricades manned by Vietnamese police and U.S. Army MPs. Guards were posted around the square and at the hotel entry. Guests were queried and cleared as they arrived. All nine Generals, and Captain K, arrived at about the same time. All were in dress uniforms for having earlier been at a formal Embassy event. Their chauffeured cars were allowed through the barricades such that they and their wives exited right at the hotel entry, to be greeted by Andre. Press photographers were snapping pictures.

The party was a huge success. It was covered in the Saigon Daily News, the Saigon Post, and the Stars and Stripes. It helped that the editors of all three were among the guests.

It was also covered, of all places, in The National Geographic, the least likely publication one would expect to cover a Navy "wetting down" party. That coverage appeared a month or two later as part of a wider story about Vietnam. Our party was cited as evidence of the contradictions then emerging in the country. It was reported as "A lavish social event, with Generals in attendance, in the roof top ball room of the Caravelle. Yet while sipping wine or whisky one could step out on to the balcony and see flames from a freighter on the river that had been attacked with mortars by the Viet Cong."

And such was the city, and the country, at that time, as the era of French cultural influence was finally ending, to be soon replaced by American influence - and active military engagement.

We, however, while well behaved when it came to entertaining, were not likely to be Admirals.

But we threw a hell of a party!

———◆———

CHAPTER
FIFTEEN

FAME

"Fame is a vapor......" —HORACE GREELEY

Just three weeks following the notable Wetting Down party, another social event of significance occurred. And it included a connection to Bach Yen.

In that December of 1964 the American involvement in the North/South conflict among the Vietnamese was increasing. Our advisory efforts were expanding; increased military aid flowed in ever increasing amounts through the port and the local political situation became increasingly volatile. There were coups and attempted coups, and nearly endless wrangling among the Vietnamese generals for political power. All this instability had continued from the overthrow of President Diem a year before, and the sustained instability was inspiring increasing terrorist activity by the Viet Cong. As further evidence of this change in environment, Bob Hope and his troupe were set to visit Vietnam for Christmas in 1964. He was noted for troop morale visits in time of conflict, starting with WWII and continuing through the Korean action. Always accompanied by beautiful starlets and female singers, as well as comedian Jerry Colonna and band leader Les Brown, Bob Hope was welcomed enthusiastically by U.S. forces in war zones.

Saigon, it seemed, was becoming a city in a war zone.

Bob Hope and his entourage were booked into the Caravelle Hotel, arriving Christmas Eve. A late dinner for the troupe was planned, commencing at 9pm. The late hour set whether to accommodate their travel arrival or a function of earlier commitments, I do not recall. But Max and I were, in any event, invited to the dinner. We had developed a fast friendship with Andre and done him some "favors" in the days since our party. Also invited were two other officer friends of ours, Kim and Chuck, who were now in charge of the Clubs & Messes operations, and with whom we had regular dealings in addressing their special needs. They had also come to know Andre well as they were charged with coordinating the overall visit for the Hope contingent. Andre had encouraged us to bring ladies, so as to add to the balance of the dinner table. Max and I, of course, invited Jacqueline and Colette, and Jackie C and Mimi, as well, to pair with Kim and Chuck. All these arrangements came about just a few days before Christmas Eve, and we much looked forward to what would be an extraordinary evening.

And then fate intervened.

There was a now well-known terrorist bombing of the Brinks Hotel at 5:45pm on Christmas Eve. It was quite a disastrous event, with several Vietnamese killed and the building extremely damaged. Being just across the square, the Caravelle felt its impact, as well, with some broken windows and other minor damage. Needless to say, this unsettled the best laid plans for the holiday evening. The first plan change was that Kim and Chuck were called to immediate duty as the Brinks housed a now very damaged officer's club. That canceled their attendance at the dinner. Max and I were not called to duty, although Max was scheduled as the regular Duty Officer for Christmas Day.

But that was already known and did not interfere with our evening. Andre assured us that the dinner was still to take place. We chose to still bring along Mimi and Jackie C, although their dinner companions would not now be joining.

As 9pm approached, Max and I arrived at the Caravelle, which now had an added security force and a closed public square that called for additional time to clear, especially with our four "dates." But clear we did, and soon found ourselves on the 10th floor of the Caravelle, yet again, but this time in a sequestered corner specially arranged for the dinner. Over brief cocktails we met personally with Bob Hope, who was a naturally charming, funny, and gracious man. He, in turn, introduced us all to Les Brown, Jerry Colonna and others in the troupe. He also introduced one "Bill," who was in a managerial position that was not quite clear. It was apparent, though, that "Bill" was a party of influence given his obvious familiarity with Bob Hope. Dinner was seated promptly. Conversation was lively, with Bob Hope treating everyone with graciousness. Les Brown became quite captivated with Jackie C. while the few other men in the entourage clearly enjoyed conversation with our other three "dates." I was seated near Bill and learned a bit more about him and his role as Bob Hope's business manager. That knowledge sparked in me a bit of a brain storm. It brought me to thinking about Bach Yen and her imminent departure for New York. Possibilities danced in my head.

A future in show business!

I proceeded to describe Bach Yen and her talents to Bill, and that our Navy officer team had successfully booked her on the Ed Sullivan show, to be broadcast in just two weeks. I also offered that she was still performing at the Moulin Rouge and, in fact, had a midnight show this very evening. I asked Bill if he and his junior colleague would like to break from the dinner for a quick visit to see her performance. Feeling like a budding promoter, I suggested, "Why, she might even fit into a future Bob Hope show!" To my great surprise, Bill agreed.

He joined me, with his junior associate, and we promptly left a little after 11pm, as dinner was finishing, to take a quickly arranged hotel car to the nearby Moulin Rouge. Max remained attending to our ladies.

I had become reasonably well known at the Moulin Rouge club, thanks to frequent visits, and we were quickly seated, just before the show was to begin at Midnight. Bach Yen was her usual superbly entertaining self, and Bill and his colleague seemed impressed. She came out to our table after her set, having seen me in the audience, and I introduced her to Bill without elaboration. He made brief small talk and then said that we really needed to return to the hotel as the hour was now quite late and the Hope crew had a big day ahead of them. On Christmas Day I dashed off a note to Larry and Glenn, now in the U.S., with a report of the affair and noted that Bach Yen was now at least known to the Bob Hope entertainment team. I offered that something might come of it when she arrived in New York. Visions of show biz fame again danced in my head!

Returning to the Caravelle, the evening was nearly ended with Bob Hope himself having retired to his room in our absence. Max and I expressed our thanks to all concerned, and escorted our many ladies to waiting cars and called it a very pleasant ending to what had otherwise become a sad day with the bombing. Bob Hope and his troupe proceeded with a Christmas Day show, followed by several other performances over the next 10 days. Then life returned to what was normal, if changing, in Saigon.

But the Bach Yen story had not yet ended as there was one more event of note.

Some 10 months later, in October, 1965, having recently returned to the U.S., I was serving as Aide to a Rear Admiral in San Diego. On an autumn afternoon the phone rang in my office, and upon answering I was surprised to hear none other than "Bill" of the previous Christmas Eve and Moulin Rouge experience. He had located me thanks to Bach Yen, with whom I had maintained causal contact. He located Larry, as well, through the same connection. Bill, it seemed, had encountered Bach Yen just a few weeks before in Palm Springs, where she was playing at a supper club. He explained that he was traveling with Bob Hope, as usual, and they were spending some time in Palm Springs. They decided to explore the local night life one evening, and visiting this particular dinner club, they found none other than Bach Yen singing. Bill had exclaimed to Bob Hope, "This is the young woman that the Navy officer was promoting last Christmas in Saigon!" Her performance was apparently impressive enough for Bob Hope to request a visit back stage after her show. Their subsequent conversation resulted in her being offered a role in Hope's forthcoming Thanksgiving Special.

Following this report of circumstances, Bill went on to invite me to come to Burbank and also be included in a to-be-determined spot on the show, which was to be taped in a week or so. A similar invitation had been issued to Larry, then in Los Angeles. Of course, we both accepted!

And so, a fortnight later, I was again in Bob Hope's presence, this time in the NBC studios in Burbank for the taping of his Thanksgiving special. Larry and I were both treated quite royally, given tours of the studios and lunch in the Commissary where other entertainment notables were seen and sometimes introduced. Bing Crosby was the featured guest, and I met him for a brief conversation, as well. He was, however, more enthralled with Bach Yen, with whom he engaged in extended conversation in French. Larry and I sat for some time with Bob Hope in the empty audience seats during the rehearsal and chatted amiably about a number of things. The day wore on, an audience was admitted, and the taping began.

Our spot on the show, it turned out, was when Bach Yen was to be introduced. Bob Hope was to say, "The Navy knows a good thing when they see it, and these young officers found our following guest while serving in Saigon." The camera was to then pan to the audience, where Larry and I were seated up front, in uniform, smiling proudly. Larry and I would enjoy our own brief moment of fame. And so it went –except that they eventually cut the "pan to audience part" to accommodate timing limitations!

The experience was nonetheless a unique and delightful one. Bach Yen went on with her subsequent career, Larry returned to business affairs, while I resumed my Navy duties with yet another Vietnam story in hand.

But there was to be no future in show business.

All fame is fleeting!

CHAPTER
SIXTEEN
CHANGES

"The times they are a-change'in...." — BOB DYLAN

The New Year of 1965 came quietly, and welcomed, after all the excitement of December. The promotion party, the dinner with Bob Hope, and the bombing at The Brinks hotel had made it a demanding month.

The preceding few months had also seen a good deal of local political turmoil. There had been a coup attempt against Vietnamese General Kahn, who himself had risen to authority in January of '64, somewhat displacing General Minh, who had taken over after the assassination of President Diem in November of 1963. (Although there was then a triumvirate of three Generals, including Minh - with Kahn seeming the dominant party.) There had also been an earlier attempt to displace General Kahn, in September, but it had been repulsed. That was largely due to the efforts of Air Marshall Ky and General Thi, who intervened on behalf of Kahn.

On the American side, retired General Maxwell Taylor had replaced Ambassador Henry Cabot Lodge as the senior diplomat. And General

Westmoreland had replaced General Harkins as the senior military officer. Both of those changes had taken place in the previous summer, not long after our arrival.

In the City, there were demonstrations and minor riots with increasing frequency. Most were instigated by Buddhists, who continued to pressure for a stronger voice in public affairs, as they were the majority, and to diminish the governing role of the Vietnamese Catholic elites, the minority, who had succeeded the French in civic leadership. The Cao Dai, a religious sect of mixed Catholic and Buddhist beliefs and liturgies, were also engaged in social disruption. And there was the increasing Viet Cong terrorist activity.

While the American military presence remained stable at about 17,000 total personnel, there were daily rumors of increases in that number, and even the prospect of U.S. combat troops.

Max and I thus entered 1965 with a clear understanding that things were changing in the character of the City as we had found it just 9 months previously. And our household changed, as well, as "Monsieur Moto" was soon detached after his one year of Vietnam service and transferred to San Francisco. We invited an Air Force Captain to fill the spot in the house. He was flying some then-secret high-altitude reconnaissance missions over North Vietnam and Laos, and shared our comfortable abode for the remainder of our days in the city.

Amidst all these changes, a quiet weekend in Cap St Jacque seemed in order, and I still had some "flight credits" with my Army pilot friends. Colette so loved the place that she was quite amiable to a visit and so it was planned for late February.

As with our prior visits, she drove and I flew. We chose to be very private this time, and avoided contact with the other guests. We did not call upon our Army doctor friend, either. We both sensed, unspoken, that something was in the air that we needed to face privately. The weekend began with an intimate dinner at a table nearest the sea on Friday evening, then coffee and liquors on the small veranda outside our room at the pension, followed by early retirement for the night.

Saturday was quiet, as well. A late breakfast with French newspapers, then a long walk on the beach. Reading most of the day with a light lunch and equally light conversation. Soft affection prevailed, but no great passion.

Then, at a catered Saturday dinner on our veranda, Colette said "Jeemee, we do need to talk seriously."

"Of course," I replied, "is everything all right?"

"With me, oui; but with us, non," she answered.

More confused than surprised, I asked her to clarify her answer.

She elaborated by saying that she had sincerely enjoyed our companionship of the last few months, and much appreciated my affection and attentions. It had helped steady her after the aborted move to Paris and then her return. Our relationship allowed her to collect herself in the comfort of our sharing time; but now, she said, it was time for her to think of her future.

"What do YOU expect, Jeemee," she said, "to marry me?"

Without hesitation I answered, "Yes!"

"Ha, ha, you silly boy!" she laughed, "I am too old for you, and have children. You need to go back home and find a nice young American girl." And with that she proceeded to announce that our relationship was ended, to be effective at the end of the weekend as we both returned to the city. A pragmatic Gallic approach if there ever was one.

That last night she was as gentle, loving, and sweet as one could ask for; and as much so as she had ever been, almost as if nothing had changed. We talked quietly through the evening, and later in bed, speculating on where our separate lives might take us. Gentle intimacy and soft love making. Then more conversation about the future over breakfast. She then drove me to the airfield, and went on her way back to the city. I was silent on the short flight, not visiting with the pilot as had been my habit.

Back home in the early evening of Sunday, I shared the news with Max. To my own surprise, I had accepted this all with no depression or any crushing sense of rejection. Colette had delivered the message in such a way that it all just flowed as though it had always been so determined.

Colette and I did not see each other again for several weeks, and then did have an encounter at a social event where she appeared in company with an older (30s) Air Force officer. She introduced me, and we all chatted in a cocktail party, small talk fashion, and then went our own ways.

It seemed that change was much the nature of the day. Political changes, military changes, household changes – and my own romantic changes. My first true love affair had come to an end, albeit with a soft landing. I was much matured for the experience. I thought of her fondly and frequently for many years to come.

I did see Colette once again, 20 years later. The encounter occurred at a Food Fair in Cupertino, California in 1984. On my way to visit a cousin living in the area, I had been asked to pick up a few items from a grocery. As I was shopping in the store, I walked past a lovely woman, in her late 40s, who I thought much looked like Colette. As I passed her in the aisle, I heard a voice behind me say "Jeemee, is that you?"

Startled, I turned back and answered "Colette?" And, indeed, it WAS her. The 1980 Dan Fogelberg song "Same Old Lang Syne" came quickly to mind, with its line "Met my old lover in the grocery store." We chatted awkwardly for a few minutes. I informed her that I was on my way to San Francisco on business, after spending the night with my cousin. We agreed that she would meet me in the city for lunch in a day or two, and she gave me her phone number.

I called late the next afternoon after arriving at my San Francisco hotel, and she came up the following day for what became a very, very long lunch. We caught up on our lives. She had married a CIA agent/employee about a year after I left Saigon. He was soon transferred back to the U.S and they had lived in the Washington D.C. area for some time, and recently moved to California where he was engaged in the early stages of Silicon Valley technology development. Her daughter was in her 20s and lived in Paris, near her father, Colette's first husband, as did Colette's younger son. The older son was an officer in the French Army and stationed in Corsica. We reminisced about Saigon, the end of the war, and mutual friends from those days. Colette was quite happy, looked marvelous, and was kind and affectionate.

For the next 3 or 4 years we exchanged Christmas cards. Then one from her did not come, and mine came back as lacking a forwarding address, and I could not find her again.

As for Max and Jacqueline, that romance was ending as well. Jacqueline was considering a move to Paris or Hong Kong as the political situation in Saigon worsened; and Max, like me, was considering his next duty station and where his life might go next. They slowly, and quietly, began to go their separate ways.

My first true love affair was truly over.

"Breaking up is hard to do...."
—Neil Sedaka

CHAPTER
SEVENTEEN
SETTING, WITH THE SUN

"Aim at the sun, and you may not reach it, but your arrow will fly far higher...." — J. HAWES

*M*ax and I had arrived, aiming for the sun, and we had benefited from our arrows flying higher. But now that sun was setting. Setting, as in the end of an era. And the Sun, in this case, also being Janney Sun. She was the strikingly beautiful Taiwanese on whom I had a momentary crush when she came to one of our dinner parties with a young CIA officer. When my romance with Colette ended, I attempted to court Janney – briefly.

The occasion was a dinner party hosted by Captain K. I tracked her down through friends and she agreed to join me as my date for the event. As it turned out, that was my one and only date with her, as Captain K himself became enthralled and specifically asked me to arrange an opportunity for him to get to know her better. Being ever responsive to those in positions of authority, I quickly agreed to a more private and extended introduction at a lunch. Thus arranged, we three gathered at the Circle de Sportif Club a few days later.

Captain K's behavior reminded me of my own when I first met Colette – clearly attracted, but showing some nervousness at the prospects.. The connection was, in the event, a success as Janney was very shortly seen on the Captain's arm at all social events and with him at the best clubs and restaurants in town.

For my part, I soon met a lovely Vietnamese/Chinese girl, Wong Tu Ha, who I took to calling "Susie Wong," taken from the popular movie of the day. Just 19 years old, studying at a French girl's academy in Saigon, she was the daughter of a wealthy Vietnamese/Chinese merchant and lived in a large, private compound with her parents and extended family. We met at a music concert at the French Embassy, where she sought me out to practice her English. A romance ensued for my few remaining months in Saigon, and continued by correspondence for a short while after I departed. Most significant, it was my first experience at racial discrimination. Her father forbade her any relationships with white men! ..... so, we had to meet with great discretion in well-arranged public venues, and otherwise confine our time to secret lunches and dinners at my house on the Rue Croix Rouge.

As for Janney, things started to get tricky. The Captain wanted her to be issued a Commissary and Exchange card, which he asked of Max. I was advised that she also was to have free run of his official car and driver, to be dispatched whenever she asked. Max and I managed the relationship cautiously in our final months in Saigon.

Captain K decided to host a surprise farewell dinner party for us just a day or two before our summer departure. Janney was to serve as hostess, with a number of senior officers attending. Max, however, had decided to take a "farewell weekend" trip to Hong Kong, with Jacqueline, just as this event unfolded. And the trip was without asking for leave!

I scampered to contact him by phone and telegram, advising to get back immediately. Successful in getting a flight, I then had Ricky meet the plane with detailed instruction as to why he was arriving at the dinner late. It all worked out and we much enjoyed and appreciated being feted by the Captain and Janney among so many senior officers.

Over time the relationship between Captain K and Janney took on tones of social scandal. Many months after Max and I left Saigon, it finally ran its course and sadly ended with Captain K facing a Court Martial at Treasure Island. Accused of many improper actions during his tenure at HEDSUPACT, including his indiscretions with Janney. It all became national news in due course. Janney was last seen staying in a hotel in San Francisco, waiting to possibly be called as a witness, when it all ended. Captain K was found guilty of some very minor charges, reduced 100 places on the seniority list, and immediately retired. The Navy certainly wanted to avert further scandal!

The entire affair with Janney was one of the originating causes of the Navy exiting its support role in Saigon, which it turned over to the Army shortly thereafter. Indeed, it was an historical aberration that the Navy held such an important and wide-ranging shore command in Saigon. There was clear reason to believe that this somewhat scandal tainted affair was but the starting point to have the Navy removed from the city entirely. Interservice rivalries did abound in the day.

As this scandal was first beginning to unfold, Max and I were ending our movie script life in Saigon and moving on to other duties in other places - the "setting" of our time in the city. Life, for most of our 15 months in Saigon, had been very much like a war according to MGM.

No longer.

When we arrived, the senior officers all had their families.

Now all the dependents were gone, sent home in February and March.

The UN Truce Observers – Canadians, Poles, and Indians – had left in February, at the instigation of Hanoi.

The Marines had landed a battalion at Danang in March, to secure the South Vietnamese air base from Viet Cong attacks, this being the first introduction of American ground forces.

Bombing raids on selected targets in North Vietnam had commenced by both South Vietnamese and U.S. air forces, such action further expanding direct U.S. participation in combat.

Political turmoil continued in the South.

By June, it was a new Vietnamese General in charge, with the U.S. now pressing General Thiu to reduce the role of Air Marshall Ky.

Uniforms had changed.

When we reported, Tropical White Short was an often used and permitted uniform (white, short sleeved shirt with shoulder boards; white Bermuda shorts; and knee length white socks with white shoes.) If not in Whites, we were in Navy Khaki uniforms, equally suitable to the weather with short sleeves.

Now we all wore combat fatigues.

As Max and I were departing, in July, the Times front page reported the first signals from the Pentagon that a call-up of Reserves was looming at home.

The Vietnam War, as we would all come to know it, was clearly underway.

And it had all arisen rapidly, over what was only a matter of months since families had been present and we enjoyed a quasi-colonial life.

Returning to the USA was not so bad at that point in time. While not welcomed like GI's in 1946, we were not yet spit upon like those who followed us in 1969 and after.

In fact, we were mostly greeted with curiosity.

What was the war all about? What was it like in Vietnam?

Most significantly, both Max and I returned as experienced young men, much matured by our time in Saigon. We had been exposed to, and participated in, a very complex social structure of politics, military commands, foreign cultures, varied experiences, and personal relationships.....all of them changing as a war slowly began.

Ever fortunate, for Max and me, duty in Saigon was now classified as being in a "war zone." As such, Max and I were entitled to preference in seeking our next duty station. Max chose the Naval Air Station in Hawaii, and I asked for duty as an Aide to a Flag Officer. That proved tricky, however, as Admirals generally choose their Aides based on personal knowledge of, or exposure to, such junior officers. I had no such exposure, having been in Saigon for 16 months, but a Rear Admiral in San Diego was impressed with my Fitness Reports from Capitan K, and agreed to take me on as his Aide.

That, too, eventually proved a life and career changing event...... but that is another book!

The sun had set on a brief era in the history of Saigon.

That era had been a time still with romance,
humor, and adventure.

———◆•◆•◆———

THE END

ABOUT THE AUTHOR

Mr. De Francia is an executive and shareholder of a national real estate development company engaged in residential, commercial, and resort projects. Prior to his private sector experience, Mr. De Francia served as a decorated officer in the U.S. Navy. Posts included Headquarters Support Activity, Saigon; Aide to the commanding Rear Admiral NSC San Diego; Office of the Chief of Naval Operations; and the U.S. Embassy, Caracas, Venezuela. He also served on several Panels and Commissions in the Pentagon, was awarded the Distinguished Civilian Service Medal, and is a retired Commander in the Naval Reserve. He is a member of The Atlantic Council and the U.S. Naval Institute, as well as The Union League Club in New York and the Army-Navy Country Club in Washington, D.C.

Mr. De Francia has lived in South America, the Caribbean, Chicago, New York, and Washington D.C. He is widely traveled having visited 67 different countries, is fluent in Spanish, and capable in Italian and French. A fourth generation native of the Centennial State, he and his wife Cynthia now live on a ranch just outside of Steamboat Springs, Colorado, where they enjoy frequent visits from their large family of seven children and seven grandchildren, as well as numerous brothers, sisters, nephews, and nieces.

For sales, editorial information, subsidiary rights information
or a catalog, please write or phone or e-mail

IBOOKS
Manhanset House
Shelter Island Hts., New York 11965, U.S.
Tel: 212-427-7139
www.ibooksinc.com
bricktower@aol.com
www.IngramContent.com

For sales in the U.K. and Europe please contact our distributor,
Gazelle Book Services
White Cross Mills
Lancaster, LA1 4XS, U.K.
Tel: (01524) 68765 Fax: (01524) 63232
email: jacky@gazellebooks.co.uk

www.ingramcontent.com/pod-product-compliance
Lightning Source LLC
Chambersburg PA
CBHW031548260326
41914CB00002B/328